"In the midst of her own pain, Sallie reached out and surrounded all who knew her with love and steadfast courage. She inspired others not only with her words but with her presence. She will live on in all of us."

Marilyn Van Derbur
author of *Miss America by Day*

"She had such a profound effect on me and on many other people. I have seen her strength, her faith and her ability to understand a person deeply and make them feel loved."

—A Survivor

"We don't know God's timetable, why He does what He does, or when He plans to do what He has planned. Life is a journey. I am so glad that He chose Sallie to be part of my life. My life is richer and fuller because of her and her family."

—A Friend

"Sallie was a true gift from God of kindness and compassion. . . . Her experiences gave her the foundation of wisdom and caring that have helped her to help many others and me."

—An Al-Anon Member

"I was impressed that she could reach out to so many people who were hurting. I know that her life at various points was hard, but I admired her fighting spirit. In fact, what I admired most is that she helped so many of us identify our demons and conquer them."

—An Al-Anon Member

"Sallie shared herself on a deep and personal level with so many people and gave her time and energy to help others. . . . She touched my heart and soul in a way that has been life changing."

—An Al-Anon Member

"Through her efforts Sallie has educated and brought light to professionals and survivors as to just how terrible sexual abuse is to the victim. The victim grows into a survivor who develops into a whole person with greater understanding and compassion for others who have experienced abuse."

—An Al-Anon Member

Sallie Engel was a survivor of childhood sexual abuse who wanted to make a difference in the way health care professionals care for children and adults who have been traumatized. In 2004 Sallie and her husband, Les, established the Sallie Engel Trauma Survivor's Education Fund with the CentraCare Health Foundation, St. Cloud, Minnesota. The fund will educate health care professionals about the long-term effects of childhood trauma on adults.

Judy Kallestad was a personal friend of Sallie Engel's for over twenty-five years. Her articles have appeared in regional publications such as *Style* and *Business Central* as well as such magazines as *Motor Home* and *Collectibles Canada*. She holds a bachelor's degree in sociology from the University of Minnesota and a master's degree in special education from St. Cloud State University.

Letters to Sara

ℰ • ℭ

A Sexual Abuse Survivor's Healing Journey

Help for Survivors and Health Care Professionals

Sallie C. Engel
with Judy Kallestad

About the Cover

The Raggedy Ann doll pictured on the cover was Sallie's recovery doll and represented her inner child, Sara. Sallie learned to nurture herself by nurturing the doll. She loved Raggedy Ann and Andy dolls and related memorabilia and had a large collection of dolls and other items. She picked Raggedy Ann as her recovery doll because she had one as a child.

ISBN: 0-9764606-0-2

Pre-press by North Star Press of St. Cloud, Inc., St. Cloud, Minnesota

Printing by Versa Press, Inc., East Peoria, Illinois

Published by:

Trinity Consultants, Inc.
927 Julie Drive
Saint Cloud, Minnesota 56303
www.trinity-consultants.org

Dedication

To God, my Father and Heavenly Parent.

To my husband of forty-one years, Les. He has been my lover, my supporter, my best friend, the father of my children, my encourager, and my champion.

To my children: Les, Richard, Kathleen, Marty, and my daughters-in-law, Stephanie and Sherry, who have supported me in every way they could during my recovery.

To Sara, my inner child, the sweet innocent child of God who did not feel wanted or accepted.

Contents

PART ONE
My Story

Finding Sara: My Wounded Inner Child
Letters to Sara
Sara, My Inner Child, The Love of My Life
Heaven Should Be Such Fun
Being Grown Up Is No Fun
God Leads Me to Good Books

The Lie: Growing Up in My Grandparents' House
Letters to Sara
Believe the Children
Make Sure Children Are Safe
You Saw a Lot of Scary Things in a Car
How Am I Supposed to Know What I Don't Know?
It's Okay to Have Feelings
What I Experienced Didn't Match What I Was Told
I Was Rejected; Then My Soul Was Rejected

Acknowledgements

Many people have contributed their time, energy, and love to help me realize my dream of writing this book. I would like to thank Thornie Lively, my cousin, who filled in a lot of blanks about my childhood.

I am thankful to the many health care professionals who have had a part in my healing: Dr. Ralph Cunningham, Dr. Bob Rafferty, Dr. Titus Bellville and his wife, Carol Bellville, Dr. Sharon Ruggiero, Steve Carr, and Dr. James Bryer.

Also, I want to thank Pastor Jerry Staehling, who has been my spiritual support, and to him I will be forever grateful. He told me when I joined the Lutheran Church that his job was not to judge me but to support me.

My heartfelt appreciation goes to Marilyn Van Derbur Atler, Miss America of 1958. She is a survivor who inspired me and taught me that you can get through difficult circumstances in your life if you just do your work.

My special thanks to Judy Kallestad and Wendy Hendricks for making this book a reality. It would never have happened had it not been for their love and dedication. I am also grateful to Mary Schnettler and the St. Cloud Area Writers Group for their help and guidance with the book and to Multimages for the cover design.

Sallie Engel

Preface

I am one of an estimated sixty million survivors of childhood sexual abuse in America today. The trauma connected with this abuse causes long-term physical, emotional and spiritual damage. According to statistics, one out of three women and one out of five men are sexually abused before the age of eighteen. It is important to note that sexual abuse occurs in families of all social status. Sexual abuse affects the survivor's health, family, and workplace. In sharing my story and journey to recovery, I hope that you, the reader, will find compassion for those who are walking the same path that I have traveled for so many years.

Definitions

The focus of this book is childhood sexual abuse, so the definitions that follow refer to children. In *Surviving Childhood Sexual Abuse*, Ainscough and Toon define **sexual abuse** as "any kind of sexual behavior by an adult with a child or any unwanted or inappropriate sexual behavior by another child." This includes sexual intercourse, oral sex, anal sex, being touched in a sexual way and being persuaded to touch someone else. It does not have to involve physical contact and can include being made to look at sexual photographs, videos, or to watch other people's sexual behavior. When the abuse occurs within a family it's called **incest**.

A **perpetrator** or **abuser** is anyone who has sexually abused a child. The perpetrator could be a family member, a stranger, an acquaintance, or another child. Statistics show that eighty percent of abusers are men. In a large percentage of cases, the perpetrator is someone the child knows, loves and trusts.

Survivors are people who have been sexually abused as children and have found ways to survive this trauma. Ainscough and Toon point out that by confronting their past and working on their recovery, many survivors have gone beyond surviving to live full and happy lives.

According to Laura Davis in *The Courage to Heal Workbook*, early literature on abuse often referred to the "victims" of abuse. The use of the word "survivor" instead conveys a sense of strength and empowerment. Another term Davis refers to is the "healing process." She states that although the stages do not take place in a particular order, "there are universal themes that emerge: deciding to heal, remembering the abuse, believing it happened, knowing it wasn't your fault, getting in touch with anger and grief, talking about the abuse, and finally moving on."

The Effects

The inability to trust others is a significant effect for those who have experienced sexual abuse. We often feel different from other people. In addition, we may feel sad, unsafe and alone. According to the article "Sexual Abuse: The Shattered Trust," "The effects of sexual abuse can be devastating. Most survivors feel an enormous sense of guilt and shame. They may feel ashamed that they didn't fight off the perpetrator's sexual advances or that they let it go on for a long time without telling anyone" (www.iEmily.com). Sexual abuse frequently happens in families where other kinds of abuse are going on, such as drug and alcohol abuse or domestic violence.

Rage is another common effect of sexual abuse when anger is repressed. Survivors may develop physical symptoms, such as sleeping problems or eating disorders. The abuse of drugs, alcohol or tobacco, as well as depression and suicide are also greater for persons with a sexual abuse history. What's important to remember is that sexual abuse is never the child's fault, no matter how the child dressed, talked or acted. It's always the abuser who has a serious problem and needs help (www.iEmily.com).

Introduction

Dear Reader,

I was born to a "reality challenged" mother and a father whose identity I never knew for sure. I grew up in my maternal grandparents' oppressive home and lived in an adult world where children were to be seen and not heard. For twenty years, I endured sexual abuse in a dysfunctional but outwardly respectable Ohio family. I learned through it all that sexual abuse has nothing to do with sex. It's all about power and control over another person.

The Letters

After reading a lot about sexual abuse through the years, I started to write down my experiences and feelings. Many survivors find that writing is therapeutic and important in their recovery. According to Ainscough and Toon in *Surviving Childhood Sexual Abuse*, "Writing can also release additional memories and feelings that have been blocked off. This can be frightening, but it is also useful in the healing process. . . . Writing isn't the same as just thinking things out. Many survivors get access to their memories and feelings and begin to understand themselves better once they begin to write."

Letters to Sara

My writings are addressed to Sara, who is my inner child or younger self, the little girl I was never allowed to be as I was growing up. I have chosen to share these very personal letters to Sara that depict my spiritual recovery journey to let other survivors know that they are not alone in their experiences and feelings.

About the Book

It is my hope that survivors will realize that by working on their recovery they can find peace. Also, I hope to educate health care professionals about the long-term effects of sexual abuse so that they can provide the compassionate care and support that survivors need.

Part One – "My Story" is a historical account of my life. Chapter One begins at a crossroads in my life and tells how I discovered Sara, my inner child. Chapters Two through Five continue my story of twenty years of sexual abuse and how as an adult I have chosen to cope with these experiences. The story of my life is interspersed with flashbacks. The letters at the end of these chapters are my therapeutic writings to Sara that I began to write thirty years after the abuse. They are really my reflections on crucial events in my life. Chapter Six is the continuation of my spiritual journey and God's role in it all. Chapter Seven concludes my story, with Sara finding a home where she is loved and accepted. The Epilogue is about my latest journey.

Part Two – includes "Resources to Help in Working with Survivors." Chapter Eight is a compilation of writings from health care professionals concerning what they have learned from working with me that could help in working with other survivors. In Chapter Nine, survivors offer suggestions to health care professionals about how to treat them to assist in their recovery. The "Appendix" contains a list of resource information and materials that I hope will be helpful to you.

God's love and peace,

Sallie Engel
August 2004

Part One

My Story

What lies behind us and what lies before us
are tiny matters compared to
what lies within us.

—Walt Whitman

Chapter One

Finding Sara

My Wounded Inner Child

I n 1991 my life began to fall apart. I was forty-nine years old, my youngest child had left for college, and I was alone with plenty of time to think. That's when memories of the sexual abuse started to flood back, and I began having flashbacks.

In the article "Safeline, Information on Flashbacks," flashbacks are described as recollections from the past. "As a child you had to protect yourself from the emotional and physical horrors of abuse. In order to survive, that child remained locked inside, unable to express the feelings and thoughts of that time. It is as though we put that part of us into a time warp until it comes out in the present. . . . Flashbacks sometimes make you feel insane because the child in you doesn't know that there is an adult survivor available to help" (www.healthyplace.com). Like many other survivors, I suffer from Posttraumatic Stress Disorder (PTSD). And like others with PTSD, I had to be in a safe place to start to deal with the traumatic memories of abuse.

In Marilyn Van Derbur Atler's book, *Miss America By Day: Lessons Learned from Ultimate Betrayals and Unconditional Love*, she says that most women work on their recovery when they are in their forties and fifties. So, before that time, I was in the survival mode not the recovery mode. I was trying to raise a family, balance my work life and wear a mask so people didn't know how hard I was trying just to keep it together.

I started seeing a psychologist. I told him I was a survivor and that I learned quickly. I said that I had a special occasion coming up soon, so he had two weeks to fix me. Now years later, I'm still seeing him.

Having grown up in an alcoholic family, I was also attending Al-Anon meetings, which offer help to families and friends of alcoholics. I believe in the Twelve-Steps program, which is part of both Al-Anon and Alcoholics Anonymous, and I try to follow it. The most important step for me was the Third Step, which talks about the God of my understanding. Here I found my connection to God, the Father and Perfect Creator.

As I began reading books, I also started challenging many of the stories and beliefs from my childhood. I became aware of Sara, my wounded inner child, my younger self, the child I was never allowed to be. I had always been looking for something to help me make sense of my childhood. When I found Sara, my life started to make sense at last. If I listened to Sara as she related stories from the perspective of my younger self, I could discover who I really was. In my mind she was a beautiful child, not a mistake, but rather the product of her dysfunctional family.

* * *

In this chapter the letters explain who Sara is to me. I invite her to come out into the warm and nurturing environment that every child deserves. I also talk about the value of reading good books to find answers.

Life begins as a quest of the child for the man and ends as a journey by the man to rediscover the child.

—Laurens Van Der Post
The Lost World of the Kalahari

Sara, My Inner Child, the Love of My Life

Dear Sara,

You are so precious and loved. I want to hold you, keep you safe and tell you about the wonderful life God has planned for you. We will do so many great things together as you grow up. You, my precious child, will have a love for life and the excitement, energy, and inquisitiveness of no other child. You are a gift from my Heavenly Father that I will cherish forever.

I want to read to you. Reading can open up a world that is so exciting and beautiful it will take your breath away. You can read just to pass the time away, and you can read to develop your mind. When you read, you discover a world that is inviting and beautiful.

Reading will prepare you for challenges and dangers, and help you know about a loving God who only wants the very best for you. My hope and prayer is for you to grow up safe. I promise to do everything in my power to protect you.

Love,

Sallie

He will wipe every tear from their eyes. There will be no more death or mourning or crying or pain, for the old order of things has passed away. —Revelation 21:4

Heaven Should Be Such Fun

Dear darling, precious Sara,

You are always with me, and you understand everything I think and feel. You are my best friend, my forever friend, and my spiritual connection to God. The Bible says that we must become like children to enter into the Kingdom of God. Wow! Heaven should be such fun. We will all talk the same language. We will all be equals, and no one will have an agenda or try to show someone else up. Nobody will be frustrated. We will all be God's children—innocent, joyful and playful.

Sara, you will be able to play and have fun. You can have a playhouse, and other children will want to play with you. It will be painted white outside and yellow inside and have a flower box on the window filled with beautiful flowers. It will be one room—a kitchen with a table to sit at and have cookies and chocolate milk. The kitchen appliances will work, and it will have running water and an icebox that you can open and close. It won't be that new plastic stuff. It will be the old fashioned kind made of metal and painted pink. You will have a tea set with cups, saucers and little plates to serve the cookies. You can have fresh lemonade sometimes instead of milk. You can have dolls, doll beds, highchairs, a baby carriage, a cradle, and a rocking chair. You can be a mom with lots of babies and lots of doll clothes to dress the babies. You can go horseback riding. You can have a cat and a dog that do tricks. I don't think there will be any TVs or electronic toys in heaven.

Little boys will play adventure games, build forts and be lion tamers with real lions. They will ride on elephants and go on long trips. They will build bridges and playhouses for the little girls. I believe that you will be able to use your imagination there. You can build a huge sandcastle on a white beach at the ocean, watch the beautiful birds and see all of God's creatures up close.

Everything will be peaceful like in the original Garden of Eden. I think it says in the Bible something about the lion will lie down with the lamb. There will be no more sickness, no more worry, no more stress. Calm music will fill the air, and it will be so peaceful. Old and young will be together but everyone will be childlike, filled with God's everlasting love. We will all live the perfect childhood as God intended. He will be the perfect parent and will say, "Well done my good and faithful servant."

Hear the music, Sara. It's the heavenly choir singing—calling us to come and sit with the Father as he tells us stories of old. We will sit and listen intently. His voice and His gentle loving face will mesmerize us.

God's love and peace,

Sallie

Sometimes the child in one behaves a certain way and the rest of oneself follows behind, slowly shaking its head.

—James E. Shapiro
Meditations from the Breakdown Lane

Being Grown Up Is No Fun

Dear Sara,

Today I need to do a little cleaning. I really would like to be neater. But then I would not have time to do all the fun things I want to do—like spending time with you and other special people. There is always work to do, and if I did all the work I need to do, I never would find time for fun.

I hate being a responsible grown-up. Being grown up is no fun. Work, work, work! Being responsible, doing stuff right, figuring stuff out—ugh, I hate it! I want to be a little kid who just does fun stuff. I want to play and figure things out about people. Who cares what the dumb house looks like? Also, if people judge me on what I look like, they are missing out. The really important thing is being there for people. Being there for you, Sara and knowing God.

I want both, Sara, free time to do the things I enjoy and a neat house. I think I'll get rid of stuff I don't need. Thanks for the insight, Sara. You always have the answer.

With my love and appreciation,

Sallie

No man can be called friendless when he has God and the companionship of good books.

—Elizabeth Barrett Browning

God Leads Me to Good Books

Dear Sara,

I'm reading a book about the crying out of the soul. It is well written and says what I want to say very well. If I had known where to look for the answers, maybe I could have gotten better sooner—emotionally and spiritually. But I had to live it so I could explain it. If you don't know what you don't know, how do you find the right book for the answers? God leads me to books after I know something, validating what I have figured out.

I wish that I had time to just sit and look at books all the time so that I could know what I don't know. Thank you, God, for leading me in the right direction. People need to share information so that others can know they are getting better and doing it right. Many of us have such poor self-esteem and self-worth that anything that helps us undo what has been done to us needs to be pursued. Let's just cuddle up with a good book today, Sara.

Love,

Sallie

Chapter Two

The Lie

Growing Up in My Grandparents' House

I grew up feeling that I didn't belong because I never really knew who I was. But I have tried to piece together events that help to identify me. In the fall of 1941, my mother, Margaret Simmerman, became pregnant. She was twenty years old and unmarried. She kept her secret until May of 1942. When she had to tell her mother, Elizabeth, and her father, Dick, about her condition, the news was not accepted with joy.

Elizabeth was enraged about the disgrace that Margaret had brought upon the family name. My grandmother, Elizabeth, better known as "E," "Liz," "Mrs. Simmerman," or "the Queen Mother," was the controlling force in the family. She made sure that everyone had their place, and she knew and decided what place they would have.

My grandmother, Liz, in about 1975.

9

Dick's job was to find some type of cover story. In June 1942, Dick, Elizabeth, and Margaret traveled to Dick's hometown to plan the cover up. Dick's brother, Frank, was called on to help with the planning. It was decided that Margaret's cousin, Jack Crockett, would be listed as the father of the unborn child. And so the lie began.

A family drinking friend, who was a retired minister, performed the wedding ceremony for Margaret and Jack along the roadside of a mountain in Virginia. It took only a few short minutes. After the ceremony, they all went to see a family friend who was a lawyer so that a document could be drawn up. The document said that Dick, Elizabeth, and Frank were legally responsible for Margaret and the unborn child, and that Jack had no legal responsibility for the "issue" of this marriage. Jack and Margaret never lived together, and their divorce decree is dated 1945. When I saw the word "issue" on one of their documents years later, I finally knew who I was. Besides being a legal term, most people will tell you that an issue is something unpleasant that they have to deal with. I was not a daughter or a granddaughter. I was something that had to be dealt with.

Margaret returned to Ohio with Dick and Elizabeth. They found a house in Milford where they lived and awaited my birth. Elizabeth had only a short time to come up with a name for me as well as a story that would keep both sides of the family happy.

I arrived on August 6, 1942, at the Good Samaritan Hospital in Cincinnati, Ohio. My birth certificate listed my father as John (Jack) H. Crockett and my mother as Margaret Simmerman. Although he agreed to marry Margaret, Jack always denied that he was my father. I was given the name Sara Margaret Crockett.

This is the story that Elizabeth invented. She had to contend with the Irish Catholic side of her family, which needed to have this baby baptized in the Roman Catholic Church. She selected my name for two reasons. First, a child needed a saint's name to be baptized in the Roman Catholic Church. Second, she could tell her family that I was named after my maternal great-great grandmother, Sarah Margaret Cadwalader. Dick's side of the family needed a different story, so Elizabeth said that I was named after my great-great grandmother, Sallie Agnes Crockett Oglesby. Nobody ever called me Sara. I was called Sallie Crockett after Dick's deceased relative; at least that's what they told his side of the family.

Sallie Agnes Crockett Oglesby (1848-1936), at about age sixteen.

I grew up with my grandparents, my mother, and her sister. I called my birth mother, "Mother," my grandmother, "Other Mother," and my grandfather, "Dad."

* * *

It's wrong to sexually stimulate me in my crib. It all started before I could even talk. At first the touch was a normal pleasurable sensation, but when the perpetrator wouldn't stop, it became very painful. Why would anyone torture me like this?

* * *

This is me in Virginia in about 1943.

We lived in a very nice house and a housekeeper cared for me while everyone worked during the week. Christmas for me always consisted of a new Madam Alexander doll and proper gifts for a young lady. I went to nursery school, parochial elementary school, and a private Catholic high school for girls. My grandmother always made sure that I had name-brand clothes. I traveled with my grandparents and saw a lot of the world. My grandmother was a hospital consultant and made good money. She lived in a hotel all week, and sometimes I would stay in the hotel with her. But much of the time I stayed home with my grandfather.

* * *

Grandfather, car, front seat, coat, sleep . . .

My body is so small it will fit in the palm of a person's hand. I'm so small that I can be placed under a chair, in a box, in a drawer, in a pocket. No one can get my hand open, it is so tight, and I am so strong. Shame, I can't look at him and tell him what I feel. If he touches me, it will feel good, but then he won't stop. I will go out of my mind. I will leave my body. He won't stop.

The word is torture, and that is what he is doing. I want to die, or I will lose my mind. I tell myself, don't relax. He can do it again if you relax. You can't have a good feeling because he will hurt you. DON'T RELAX, KEEP YOUR BODY TIGHT SO HE CAN'T GET IN. Don't be face up. If you relax, that is very bad. Always be on your stomach; then he can't get you.

Please fix me. Just take the pieces of the puzzle and put them together and fix me. Undo what he did to my body. PLEASE! I DON'T WANT TO TALK ABOUT IT! JUST FIX ME, PLEASE.

* * *

Me at about age five in Virginia.

I knew at a very early age how to go to the hotel dining room, order my food, add on the tip and charge it to the room. I saw the inside of a Playboy Club before I was sixteen. I sat through boring business dinners and learned to sit quietly like a proper young lady should. I acquired a taste for shrimp and lobster while my peers were enjoying hamburgers and fries. A "Shirley Temple" was the beverage that a proper young lady would order when the adults ordered drinks before dinner. My grandfather taught me to play a wicked game of Canasta. His favorite saying was, "It is no game for a blind man." The message was that this is not just a game—this is serious so don't make mistakes. Pay attention and remember who played what and when. I was a great hostess and could make pleasant cocktail chatter at a very young age. I was a miniature adult, never a child, and always a perfect lady.

One of my teachers, who taught at La Salette Academy in Covington, Kentucky, in the 1950s, wrote the following in her contribution to this book, "On one occasion I felt concern when Sallie told me that her grandfather had bought her a new outfit to wear when she served as his companion at a social gathering in Cincinnati. I felt that she should not be pushed into adult society." Perhaps others noticed the unusual role I played in my grandfather's life but at that time they considered it inappropriate to investigate.

My school photo from La Salette.

15

Letters to Sara

* * *

The letters in this chapter are about the physical, emotional and sexual abuse I suffered as a child growing up in a dysfunctional family. The parts of the letters that are in italics are from the perspective of my younger self, Sara's voice, as she relives some of her experiences.

A man's spirit sustains him in sickness, but a crushed spirit who can bear?

—Proverbs 18:14

Believe the Children

Dear Sara,

I was so full of shame, fear, terror and pain, yet I could tell no one what was going on in my life. I still remember the bad things, and still I'm filled with shame and fear. Can anyone make the pain go away? Who will believe the children who experience torture and terror?

I came from a good family with money and respectability in the community. We were churchgoers and I attended private schools. Everyone thought that I had everything a little girl could want. But I wanted someone to rescue me and take me out of the hell that I walked in every day. Instead the perpetrators said, "You are so lucky that we let you live here. Look at all the pretty things we give you. Look at all we do for you."

Believe the little children. Don't make another child live a life like mine. God, you let me repress the memories, and now I must remember and feel the pain. Sara, you're a fighter who won't die, and now you're determined to be heard.

Together we'll tell our story, Sara, and maybe the world will listen.

Love,

Sallie

Children are like wet cement. Whatever falls on them makes an impression. —Haim Ginott

Make Sure Children Are Safe

Dear Sara,

When you were a little girl your mother would send you to the grocery store. This is what you are telling me about the man who worked there:

"He is scary. He is foreign and talks loud and has whiskers. He is always in the grocery store by himself. Liz likes him and thinks he has good stuff. Margaret sends me to the store to get bread. It is scary walking under the bridge close to the cars. Then, I have to go into the grocery store. This time the bread man is in the store too, but he does not protect me. The loud-voiced man follows me around the store. He will not let me get away. His face is scratchy. I don't like to be touched or held tight by the man with the whiskers. I can't understand his words. He speaks differently and is hard to understand.

Liz says he is nice and why should I be afraid of him. She says that he will not hurt me. She doesn't know anything. Some people are bad and should not be around little girls or boys. I want to leave. He will not let me leave. He holds me tight. Finally, I walk under the bridge and go home. Please, don't make me go back to the store. Some things are scary, and you should not let children be in a place that is scary.

Don't touch little boys or girls if they say no. NO is a word, and you better listen to it because if you don't, when I grow up, I will hit you really hard and shout, "NO, NO, NO," really loud in your ear. I'll break your eardrum because I will yell NO so loud. When I grow up, I will never tell little girls not to be afraid or that they have to like someone because I know all about bad people. Little kids know about bad people. Parents should watch out for the bad people and the bad kids. They have to make sure the little children are safe."

Sara, it is hard sometimes to tell the bad guys from the good guys. Some people are just plain bad, so families need to listen to their children and protect them.

Love you,

Sallie

We are not bitter, not because we have forgiven but because there is so much to be done that we cannot afford to waste valuable time and resources on anger.

—Govan Mbeki
Johannesburg (South Africa) *Weekly Mail*

You Saw a Lot of Scary Things in a Car

Dear Sara,

Your grandfather was a very angry driver. When you were little, you saw a lot of scary things in a car. He would wake you out a sound sleep with his yelling and cussing. Your stepfather, Bill, was not a safe driver either.

Sara, this is what you are telling me: *"Cars are not safe for little girls. A person who is angry should not be allowed to drive a car. Angry people should be put in a box, locked up and never let out. It is not nice to scare little kids."* Wow, I have a headache again just thinking about these experiences.

Sara, I am so sorry about all the angry people who scared you when you were little. You didn't have any place to run or anyone to protect you. Now I'll keep you safe, and I won't let angry people hurt you ever again. Don't be scared, Sara. You're safe now. All the bad people are gone. God loves you, and He will watch over you just as He did when you were little. It's okay to cry now. You can let all the scary feelings out because I will listen and you are safe.

Love,

Sallie

How does a man become wise? The first is to trust and reverence the Lord.
                                                    —Proverbs 1:7

How Am I Supposed to Know
What I Don't Know?

Dear Sara,

I remember when you were a little girl you used to go fishing with your grandfather. He would put on his wading boots and go off into the water. You were supposed to stay on the shore and pretend you were fishing and just be good. Many times he was gone for quite some time out of sight. One time you had shorts on and ran through some sticker bushes. I remember that it hurt a lot. You did not understand why your legs hurt or what had happened. It was very scary. Your grandfather was not around. People came from a house nearby because you were crying so loudly. They saw you run through the sticker bushes and knew you were hurt. They were nice people.

When your grandfather came back, he was mad that you had run through the sticker bushes. He thought that you should have known better and that you should not have made such a fuss. You didn't know why you had to go along on a fishing trip when he was fly-fishing. I'm sure having you tag along was not his idea of fun.

He made you feel like an unwanted burden and like he resented your existence. He expected you to know about things that no one had ever bothered to tell you. This made things very scary. How are you supposed to know what you don't know? Sara, I remember that you would pay attention, but you could not figure out how to know what you didn't

21

know. How could you even ask a question to find out what you didn't know? Even today it makes me tired trying to figure out what I don't know. If I knew the answer, I'd know what I need to ask. Life is backwards for me. Give me the answer, and then I will know the question.

Sara, you survived all of this so that I could live. I'm forever grateful.

Love,

Sallie

Feelings are everywhere—be gentle.   —J. Masai

It's Okay to Have Feelings

Dear Sara,

Stuffing my feelings inside has had a bad effect on my health. When feelings from your childhood come out, they make my blood sugar go very high. Also, they give me a bad headache, so I think my head is going to explode. I think you have lots of intense feelings—sadness, anger, and rejection. I am the channel that you have to work through, and it's okay. We will get through this together. I am glad that I can listen and tell your story. I love you, Sara, and I'm sorry for all the bad things that happened to you when you were little. Remember we are safe, and God is going to help us on our journey.

What's wrong today, Sara? You seem scared. I hear you saying, *"I don't know why, but I am just scared. Big people scare me because they hurt me and get mad at me. They make the rules and don't even tell me what the rules are. I'm supposed to be a mind reader and know all the rules. If I don't obey the rules, they will get mad, and they will puff up and yell at me. That scares me, and I don't like it. I get mad because I did nothing wrong. It's not nice to make up rules and not tell me. I can't get mad because then they get even madder, and they might hurt me. They could hit me, twist my arm or switch me on the legs. I hate them. When I grow up, I am going to make all the rules, but I will tell everybody the rules so they know what they are. Then everyone can obey the rules and everybody will be friends.*

The rules for little people can't be the same as the rules for big people. Little people are not little adults; they are just little

people. They sometimes are silly, but that is just because they are little people. Little people have feelings, and that's okay. Everybody gets to have feelings. Big people can't play God, and they can't control feelings. I am mad that I did not get to have feelings when I was a little girl. All my feelings are stuck inside, and I don't know how to get them out. They're good and bad feelings, but they are all stuck inside me. I wish I knew how to unlock them."

Sara, thank you for sharing your feelings. I know it's hard to show them now. It's okay to be mad at the people who hurt you when you were little. You were not loved or treated with compassion or caring. Your feelings have been stored away deep inside you for a very long time. You have to find safe people who will listen to your story and remind you it is okay to have feelings.

God loves you and so do I,

Sallie

Distrust all in whom the impulse to punish is powerful.
—Friedrich Nietzsche

What I Experienced Didn't Match What I Was Told

Dear Sara,

Remember when you were little and were told that the church was so great and the priests were not just connected to God, they were just like God? You were told how it was the only true church, and anyone who did not belong was going to Hell.

The rules were so strict that no human being could possibly follow them. How could a small child follow a rule such as not taking even a sip of water before communion? Remember how careful you had to be before communion? Instead of being happy to receive your First Communion, you were afraid. It was drilled into your head how unworthy you were and what a terrible sinner you were. You were seven years old and had supposedly reached the age of reason. But you were too young to know the difference between right and wrong

Your grandparents did things that you as an innocent child thought were wrong. But who could you tell about all the wrong things you had seen? Who would believe you? How could they be sinners as they sat in church in the second row on the left every Sunday morning? Your grandmother even had a cousin who was a monsignor, which was better than being a priest.

As a child, you tried to make the world right. What you saw and what you heard did not match up with what the church said. The church-going people said that you had to be perfect. You could not sin, but they did not do everything right either. You were so little and so confused, trying so hard to keep things straight in your head. It was like a Rubik's cube. Just keep moving the pieces around, and someday it will be perfect.

No, Sara, it never became perfect. Your world was a world of evil, distrust, abandonment, and no love. You were not crazy. You were just a little kid trying to make sense out of a very bad situation. You don't have to live there or even visit there anymore, although you may have times when certain triggers take you back there.

You are safe with me and God now. We live in an imperfect world, but we can also see love, acceptance, and good news. Sara, remember that God loves you, and so do many others. Today I'm here to listen to how it was and tell you I am so sorry. It should never have happened to you.

Sara, you are loved,

Sallie

The tongue that brings healing is a tree of life, but a deceitful tongue crushes the spirit. —Proverbs 15:4

I Was Rejected; Then My Soul Was Rejected

Dear Sara,

I know that you still have anger about the way that the Roman Catholic Church treated you. Not as much anger as you used to have, but the anger still comes out. I wonder if it will ever go away. Being rejected by a biological family and then later by the church was very hurtful. You, the child, were rejected and then, later in life, your soul was rejected. That was pretty scary. You thought that God had rejected you, that God did not want any part of you. That was the message you got.

Those men in black made up the rules, were the judges and jury and were your connections to God. That was very frightening for you as a little girl. You saw them break the rules with your own eyes. They were really good at making you feel ashamed and guilty. That's how they controlled their flock. They stole your brain, your self-esteem, and your relationship with God. That's easy to do with a vulnerable little girl, a child who was abandoned by her family.

They told you by their actions that you were not acceptable to God. Not talking to a child is a cruel form of punishment. It's as if the child does not exist and that she has no value. I am here to tell you that they were wrong. You do have value. You are a precious child of God, and He loves you. The men in black were not God. They may have thought they were, but I am here now to tell you they were not.

God loves you, Sara. You are His special child. He wants only the very best for you. Some day those men in black will have to answer to God for what they have done. Guess what? God knows everything, so they will not be able to deny what they did. I do get angry for what they did to you, and I don't want it to happen to anyone else. I'm going to try to remember that God, our Heavenly Father, is the judge and jury for everyone, including the men in black. Let's try to let Him take care of that problem, and you and I will concentrate on the good news that God loves us. Have a good day, Sara.

Love,

Sallie

Chapter Three

Alone with My Demons

Life with My Mother and Stepfather

My mother, Margaret, married again in 1949, and I got a new name. This time it was Sallie Preston. My stepfather never adopted me; they just gave the "issue" a new name and didn't care whether or not I knew who I was.

My mother, Margaret, and I in the late forties.

When Margaret and her husband, Bill, and their six young sons moved into a home of their own, I went with them. We lived in that house for a year before Bill lost his job, and we lost the house. Then back we went to live with my grandparents. My grandparents' home had three floors. On the first floor was the kitchen and living area. On the second floor there were four bedrooms. Margaret, Bill, and their boys lived on the third floor. I lived in the guestroom on the second floor. When my grandfather had business associates over, I slept in my grandmother's twin bed in his room. The first floor was mine to roam, and I spent many lonely nights doing so when my grandfather was out.

Soon we moved again, this time to a house in the country. I was never really part of Margaret and Bill's family, but I was taken along to live with them. The house frequently had no heat and had water you could not drink. Margaret worked for her mother and was gone a great deal. At night, when she was gone, I took care of the boys. I fed them, changed their diapers, and did all the things a mother would do. I learned new skills such as talking to bill collectors, opening the door to people with a summons and how to live on welfare. Sometimes, I would visit my grandparents and see the old life, and then I would have to go back to the new life.

* * *

A child has no voice . . .

    The men in my stepfather's office make fun of me, and it is not a safe place. They have pinup calendars, and it is dark, dirty and scary. I hate going to my stepfather's office. He is a scary person too.

    I don't want to see anyone or I will cry. It is scary and not safe. I don't want to remember. It is too scary, and I just cry and cry. How can I protect myself? I can't scream; no one will believe me. They will think I am crazy and that I am making up stories. I have no voice, but my mind is alert.

    This is what it is like for me with no one to talk to. I am so confused about what is going on in my body. I am trapped and afraid.

* * *

    I began having chest pains as a teenager, and a doctor gave me Valium to take away the pain, but it never really worked. I prayed hard to God to take me home. I was so alone and in such great pain. I learned to endure and not feel anything. I learned to do what I was told, when I was told.

* * *

That's me on the left at a high school dance around 1960.

No one will believe what my cousin is doing to me . . .

    I fear everyone will abandon me, if they know what he is doing to me. I am fifteen; why can't I fight him off? He is just a few years older than I am, but he is the one the family is so proud of. No one will believe me. He is stronger and more articulate than I am. He has talent. He's in a military school. I'm the little kid who does not even know who her father is. I'm the misfit. He is from a proper family, and all the relatives think that he does everything right. God knows what he's doing. I'm the one with the horrible secret.

* * *

    The following letters are reflections about life with my mother and stepfather. I longed for their love but they had none to give. I felt empty, worthless and disconnected from people. Sara's voice cries out in many of these letters as she relives some horrific experiences.

*The hardest thing for me was understanding that letting go did-
n't mean letting go of people, places, and things. It was letting go
of my ideas about how life should go. . . . An illusion I had about
being able to control my life disappeared.*

—Melody Beattie

Our Heavenly Father Is the Only Perfect Parent

Dear Sara,

I remember all the crazy things you tried to get your
mother's attention. You worked so hard to please her. I remember when you were a teenager, and she pushed you
away. She said, "Stand on your own two feet, and don't lean
on me. Don't touch me." That hurt so bad. It was a message
that she didn't want you.

I remember how you searched for your father. Your
dream was that he was going to show up at the door and be
a combination of Bing Crosby and Clark Gable. He was
going to say, "I always loved you, but they kept me away."
He was going to take you in his arms, and everything would
be okay. All the hurt and pain of your childhood would melt
away because you would have someone to love you.

That bubble burst when your aunt took you to the
stockyards after you had children of your own. She pointed out
a tall, thin, weathered old man who she said was your mother's
cousin, Jack Crockett, and your father. What a disappointment
that was. You woke up from your dream and let go of the hope
of how it was going to be. In talking to other family members,
I learned that he always denied being your father. There were,
in fact, many possible fathers, and you will never know for sure
who the *sperm donor* was. Today it doesn't matter, but as a child
it was very important. You wanted to fit in and be like everyone
else. You wanted a dad like on the *Father Knows Best* show—the
dad that called his little girl "Princess."

For you to get over the deep pain and hurt of not
knowing who your dad was, you separated "daddy" from

"Father." Daddies are earthly creatures. Some people have them, some don't. But, we all have a Heavenly Father, our Creator—who is much more than our earthly *sperm donor*. The Creator, it says in the Bible, is God the Heavenly Father, who makes us in His image and loves us unconditionally. He is the perfect parent who is always ready to listen at any time, not judge but comfort, guide and fill us with His love. As a child, Sara, you needed an earthly daddy, but as an adult you have come to realize the importance of your Heavenly Father. He brings you peace and fills you with His never-ending love.

Looks like it is going to be another beautiful day—a gift from your Heavenly Father. Let's enjoy life today.

Love,

Sallie

A baby is born with a need to be loved—and never outgrows it.
—Frank A. Clark

Accept the Pain, God Has Better Things in Store for You

Dear Sara,

You tried so hard to get your earthly parents' attention. You hoped for a Norman Rockwell family. You thought that if you worked harder and did more, they would accept you. You finally realized that they had no love for themselves, so they had none to give you. They provided food and shelter but not nourishment for your soul.

As a teenager the pain of not being connected to people caused a pain in your chest. You were born with a soul filled with love. Your parents were to nurture it, but because they couldn't do it, your soul began to wither and die. You felt empty, without value, love, or joy. You begged God to take you home. Depression, self-loathing and illness took over.

Fortunately at that time, God sent a woman into your life who believed in you, nurtured you and built you up. She was a replacement for what you needed from your parents. She was a part of your life for about ten years. When she left, your soul was no longer empty because you had learned to accept and love yourself. She nurtured the child in you and brought your soul back to life.

Sara, I know that I can rely on God to bring people into my life—some for a short time, others for longer periods of time to nurture me and help me grow on my spiritual journey. Until I felt the pain of what I missed in my childhood, I wasn't able to accept the joy of what God has to offer. As the saying goes, "No pain, no gain." I hear your pain, Sara. I cannot take it away, but I can encourage you to believe that if you accept the pain, God has better things in store for you.

People will come into our lives to help us grow, and we will be filled with God's love and peace.

Let me hold your hand, Sara,

Sallie

Flashbacks are vivid memories in which a person feels he or she is re-experiencing a past event. During a flashback, the survivor feels as if she is a child again and relives her abuse.

—Ainscough & Toon
Surviving Childhood Sexual Abuse

How Could It Have Happened and I Not Remember?

Dear Sara,

What you are telling me today is terrible to think about, but you will no longer be silent. You are saying, *"Do you believe me? It's the summer of 1957, and we are living with Dad (my grandfather) and Liz. A man named Tom is working for Dad. I have the bedroom at the top of the steps. I wake up, and I don't have my nightgown on anymore. I can't figure out why, and I tell Margaret and Bill. They say that people do strange things in their sleep sometimes. It bothers me that I don't have my nightgown on. Someone is in the bed with me; someone is taking off my nightgown and touching me. I think it happened more than once. He's strong. I'm afraid of Tom, but Bill and Margaret think he's great. Oh, God, how could you let that happen?"*

How could that have happened and I not remember? I can accept the other stuff that happened in my childhood because it wasn't rape. If this was rape, it is so much worse. I cried out last night and screamed, "Oh, God, anything, but don't let me have to say I was raped."

I thought if I was raped, no one would like me or ever want to be my friend again. I would have to tell someone if it really happened. Why would God let me have these feelings and this awareness if it didn't really happen? How could I know or even think of what it could be like if it didn't happen to me.

God only gives me as much as I can handle. This would be a hard awareness to accept. It would be like it just happened right now and not that it happened when I was fifteen. I am in a safe place now, and I will be able to deal with it, but I think I'll need people to say they are sorry it happened. God help us, Sara. I believe that it did happen, and there is nothing more horrible than rape.

Love,

Sallie

The human capacity to fight back will always astonish doctors and philosophers. It seems that there are, indeed, no circumstances so bad and no obstacles so big that man cannot conquer them.

—Jean Tetreau

Rape Is a Terrible Word

Dear Sara,

Rape it is a terrible word. It is not always intercourse as it says in the dictionary. It is a violation of a person's body and her space by another human being. It is so ugly, so degrading that she feels she must scrub and scrub her body to get it clean from being so violated.

Sara, I hear what you are telling me about being raped: *"I hold my body tight so the anger of the act cannot get in. The anger of the act produces an essence that attacks my body and seeps in through my skin. It does not matter if the perpetrator is able to pry me open and get in. His mere essence seeps in through my skin. I am powerless to keep it out. The sticky goo is everywhere, and I feel it on me. I try to jump away, but he left his mark on the sheets and on my skin. My body is tight, so the goo won't get in through any opening, but it punctures my skin, and I feel attacked by the essence. I can't escape, I can't get it off.*

My body screams out to be released, but I carry it with me forever. I am able to learn, to cope and function in society, but the terrible secret is held in my body. I pray no one will be able to see what was done to me. I feel shame knowing that if someone finds out, they will ostracize me from society. People don't know what to say. They are so repulsed when they find out it happened to me."

My dear Sara, I will hold you, comfort you and tell you I love you. It should never have happened. I love you, God loves you, and that is all that matters. I have good medical people in my life that believe me and are trying to find ways to release the body pain and memories. The physical effect on my body has taken its toll—elevated blood sugar, rectal pain, chest pains, and headaches that are so painful I think my head will explode. Numerous other memories that my body has stored have taken a toll on my body.

We are fortunate, Sara, that we have medical people who believe us and work hard to find ways to help us heal. We are getting better, but we both know we will only be able to heal with God's help.

Love,

Sallie

*Those who know your name will trust in you, for you, Lord, have
never forsaken those who seek you.* —Psalm 9:10

My Soul Cries Out in the Dark

Dear Sara,

I am sixty-one years old now, and the feelings have
returned, the haunting reminders of the child who was all
alone. My body reminds me of the past, the pain that I want
to forget. It's a strong pain that will not be still. It will tor-
ment me until I listen.

Sara, you will no longer be quiet and this is what you
are saying: *"My soul cries out in the dark, still night. I am in
pain. I am alone, no one to comfort me, no human touch can I feel.
I have been alone since I was a baby. Now as a teenager, I am
awake with my aloneness. My chest hurts, and I cannot cry the
pain is so bad. I must be silent. I must keep my pain inside because
no one will listen, no one cares. It is dark in my room as I lay in
my bed. I am cold in the winter, never able to be warm—and hot
in the summer, never able to be cool. The lack of human touch or
voice brings great pain. My body knows the pain of being alone but
my mind blocks it out. Valium is the doctor's answer for the pain.
A drug cannot kill the pain, but it will put the body to sleep. The
pain will rest in the body forever, quietly waiting to be heard."* The
past continues to haunt me.

Love,

Sallie

Courage is being scared to death—and saddling up anyway.
—John Wayne

I Shake Uncontrollably, Trying to Let Go of the Terror

Dear Sara,

I feel like I have lost a week of my life between the flashbacks and a viral infection. I have to force my brain to concentrate and force the thoughts into words. It is not a natural flow; it is so much work. The wounded child and the adult are all in one. I am in the world but not really a part of it.

Simple jobs at work, such as balancing the checkbook, sending e-mails or carrying on a conversation, are overwhelming. Neither the wounded child nor the competent adult is in control. I'm not a functioning adult running at full power.

I know this will pass. It happens at different times. The feelings of guilt and shame creep in, and I want to push myself so people will not think badly of me. People don't understand. They think I'm lazy, dumb or stupid. They have no clue about what it is like to be trapped in my body with the terror of my childhood that I need to release. Like an animal that has been terrorized that shakes to rid itself of the negative energy, I shake uncontrollably, trying to let go of the terror that I have no words to describe.

Love,

Sallie

Chapter Four

My Ticket Out of Hell

Marriage, Kids, and the
Survival-Mode Years

In the spring of 1961, a woman I worked with at a local department store told me about her son, Les (also called Ben), who was a student at the University of Cincinnati. Soon she arranged my first date with my future husband. He was a big college man, and I thought of myself as "a nursery school drop out." What a match we were. On our first date, we doubled with another couple and went to see a movie. I was not impressed with him. First he held my hand when we crossed the street. Then the following day when he took me out driving around, he brought me home and gave me a kiss on the cheek. I stormed into the house saying that I would never go out with such a fast guy again.

But we became phone friends until August 1961, when my birthday was coming up. I'd had the previous experience of not having a date for my birthday and having my mother give some guy twenty bucks to take me out. Since I didn't want that to happen again, I agreed to another date with Ben. We dated every day for a couple of months, and then he gave me his class ring and asked me to go steady. I had never gone steady, and so in a few weeks I asked him when we were going to get married. To this day Ben jokes about how our going steady turned into a marriage.

When I went to get our marriage license, I found out that my stepfather, Bill Preston, never adopted me, so I

Ben and I on our wedding day (June 15, 1963), Sharonville, Ohio.

wasn't actually Sallie Preston. Margaret said to make sure I told them at the license bureau that my name was Sallie Crockett. As usual, she never gave me a reason but just that this is what I was to tell them.

On June 15, 1963, I married Ben. I walked down the aisle and there, much to my surprise, stood the man who had asked me to be his wife. I never really believed he would be there. But this poor man did not have a clue as to what he was going to learn about me.

Our honeymoon was a one-night disaster. I took all my beautiful nighties along to have a fashion show. What else do you do on a honeymoon? After the fashion show, I crawled into bed. When Ben sat down on the bed, I jumped eight rigid inches off the bed. Needless to say, nothing exciting happened on our honeymoon, and we returned home the next day.

The following Wednesday we went to see my family doctor, who prescribed more Valium and a shot to help me to relax. On Saturday we went to see Ben's family doctor, Dr. Ralph Cunningham. With the help of hypnosis, Dr. Cunningham realized I had a secret. He was the first of many fine medical people to whom I will always be grateful. I was not ready at that time in my life to share with him or anyone my history of sexual abuse. He guided me through the first ten years of my marriage.

Our first child, Lou, was born in 1965 and passed away at the age of seven months. We did not have a church service when he died. I was refused absolution because I confessed to a priest back then that I was practicing birth control when our son was sick. I don't blame the priest because he was just following the rules and doing his job. But it never felt right not having a church service for Lou. Ben and I had four more children—Les, Dick, Kathleen, and Marty. They were born two years apart so I was always busy nursing a baby or getting ready to have a new one. We had a busy, active life with our children.

Memories of my long-repressed childhood sexual abuse began coming back in the 1980s when I was a middle-

Our family in 1989. Left to right: front row: Dick, me, Kathleen, and Lester; back row: Ben and Marty.

aged adult. I went to my family physician and told him that I was an unfit wife and mother. He asked me, "Did anything ever happen to you that you never told anyone about?" For the first time, I revealed to him the abuse. He told me that I had to tell my husband. I thought that if Ben knew he would throw me out. Of course, he didn't, and we started seeing a Twin Cities counseling couple. Two years of counseling with them was just a band-aid fix that got us through the teenage years with our kids.

In 1989 I began attending Al-Anon group meetings. These groups taught me how to deal with having grown up in an alcoholic family and also how to forgive those who had sexually abused me and those who could not protect me.

In 1991, I was able to have a memorial service to commemorate the death of our son Lou, who had died back in 1965. At last I was able to put closure to this part of my life.

I have been working daily on my recovery since February 1991. I've come a long way, and I'm getting better every day. There were days when my brain was out to lunch. I was in a fog and could not remember simple tasks. Some days I was physically present, but mentally I was nowhere to be found. Recovery has given me back my brain. The abusers took it, and I have to work each day to get it back. I love having a brain. I am like a child who is discovering a new world.

* * *

The next letters are about some crucial events in my life. They are about Lou and how his death and my early life experiences affected how I raised my other four children. Also, there are letters about the death of my only granddaughter, Emily, and my daughter-in-law, Sherry. In the last letter, I reflect on how quickly time has passed.

Children are a gift from God; they are his reward.

—Psalm 127:3

God Loaned Lou to Us for Seven Months

Dear Sara,

I remember the birth of our first son, Lou. I can easily replay the week he died, but maybe this time I can look at the week he was born.

Ben and I awaiting Lou's birth, spring 1964.

I woke up Sunday morning, and my water had broken. It was a slow leak. We lived in an upstairs apartment in Greenhills, Ohio. I called Dr. Cunningham to tell him, and I remember saying that I didn't wet the bed. The water just kept coming out. I stayed in bed, and Ben kept washing towels and putting warm towels under me so the bed would not get wet. Later, some friends stopped by to see us, and I think I remember eating a huge strawberry sundae. We stayed around the house until evening. I remember going to the hospital but not as we had planned. Ben was in Bermuda shorts, and I was in a one-piece mu mu dress.

The room they took me to was dark, and patients had to sit on a portable commode that was in the room. It was nothing like the way they do it now. I think Ben came in to see me for a short time, and then he went back to the father's waiting room. The next thing I remember was waking up late

Monday afternoon in bed in a room with three other women. I didn't know what was going on, I'd been asleep for a long time. I had roses beside my bed. Lou was there, I was a mom, and it was so unreal.

Back in those days a new mother stayed in the hospital for about a week. The nurses waited on you hand and foot, and they brought the babies in at a certain time to be fed. Finally, you got to get your little one all dressed up in some stiff, fancy suit, and you rode out in a wheelchair, and off you went home.

At home Ben was in charge of making baby formula. The kitchen was like a lab, everything so clean and sanitary. If Lou dropped his pacifier, it had to be sterilized before it went back in his mouth. Everyone watched his every move. After all he was the first Engel grandchild. For seven months he was part of our life. He never walked, talked or sat up, but he could smile, and he was ours. That all happened thirty-nine years ago. It was another life, another time.

I have often thought of how it would have been if he had been healthy and lived, but that's a dream. The reality is that God loaned him to us for seven months. It would have been devastating to have to put him in an institution when the day came that physically I could no longer care for him. I took care of him for seven months until his Heavenly Father took him home. His little body would never have to struggle again for air—he was at peace. Thank you, God, for the birth of this precious child, so we could know about life and death early in our marriage. Happiness and sorrow—they are a part of earthly life. It is a lesson we needed to learn early in our marriage.

Love,

Sallie

If I rise on the wings of the dawn, if I settle on the far side of the sea, even there your hand will guide me, your right hand will hold me fast. —Psalm 139:9

Closure on Lou's Death at Last

Dear Sara,

I want to thank you for all you have taught me and how you have helped me through the most difficult of times. June 22, 2004, would have been Lou's fortieth birthday.

Lou was important to many people. When he died, all I can remember is that I was at peace. I knew he would never be in pain again. I was the one who was with him most of the time when he would gasp for air. He was so helpless, frail and fragile. When he would have an attack, I would hold his limp little body, but I was helpless to make him better.

I now know why I was at peace when he died— because I had you, Sara. I knew how much you had suffered when you were little. Children don't have the words to tell you how afraid they are and how much pain they're in. It was previously thought that babies had no feelings or sensations. Medical procedures were done on small infants without any pain medication.

I could look in Lou's eyes and see the fear and the terror. He didn't know what was happening to his small body when his throat would collapse. He could not breathe for medical reasons, but, Sara, you could not breathe because of what another person did to you. You wanted to die, too, to stop the pain.

I was able to let Lou go because I knew he would never be in pain or be afraid again. He was at peace. You, on the other hand, have told me your story of fear, terror, and sadness in many ways. I now understand, and I'm so sorry for your pain. You did not deserve to be tortured. You were a small, helpless little girl, and adults took their anger out on you. God loved you so much, and He let you live so I could tell your story.

Because Lou died, I was determined never to let God take another of my children. I took them to see a doctor six weeks before they would sneeze. I was the over-protective mother when it came to health issues, and I guess everything else concerning them. I never realized how much I wanted to be in control of everything around me. Sara, you taught me well. Be vigilant, on guard and always watching so nothing bad will ever happen again.

Love,

Sallie

When you are a mother, you are never really alone in your thoughts. A mother always has to think twice, once for herself and once for her child.   —Sophia Loren
Women and Beauty

I Can't Control Whether My Children Live or Die

Dear Sara,

I never realized I had a control problem until I went to Al-Anon. There I learned it is quite common for children of alcoholics to want to be in control. They think they can control the alcoholic. I thought that if I was in control, nothing bad could happen again. I was even going to control whether my children lived or died. Finally, when I realized I could not control their living or dying and that it was up to God, it made life a lot easier. I figured out what I could control. I could control how my child would be buried and what kind of a service I could have for him.

When Lou died, I was still a member of the Roman Catholic Church. The first time he got sick, I ran to church to confession, like all good little Catholics did back in the sixties. I thought that I must have done something bad, and God was punishing me by making him sick. Wanting to be truthful, I told the priest I was practicing birth control. The rules of the church in those days forbade birth control. When the priest asked if I was going to stop practicing birth control, I said, "No."

My doctor's advice was not to become pregnant again. I trusted my doctor more then the priest, so I said that I would not stop practicing birth control. With that, the priest refused me absolution. This meant I was not welcome to receive the sacraments. So, I was a mom without a church home when Lou died. We did not have a church service for him. In fact, the priest would not even come to the hospital the night he died. He said there was no need since Lou was just a baby. I guess he wasn't concerned about a baby because Lou had been baptized. So, in the priest's mind, there was no problem. Baptized babies go to heaven. I think that I was the one who could have used some sort of spiritual comfort at the time. That had been my problem all along. I needed to have a church service for my son.

In February of 1991, a Lutheran pastor, along with my friend, an Episcopal pastor, helped me plan a beautiful memorial service for Lou. Even though no one in St. Cloud knew our son or us at the time he died because we lived in Cincinnati then, over fifty people who were Twelve Step friends of mine came. Finally, in St Cloud, Minnesota, in February of 1991, I could finally put spiritual closure to our first son's death. Sara, I will always hold Lou in my heart.

Love and Peace,

Sallie

IN MEMORY OF
LOUIS FREDERICK ENGEL
June 22, 1964   February 2, 1965

God grant me the serenity
To accept the things I cannot change,
Courage to change the things I can,
And wisdom to know the difference.

A boy is a son until he takes a wife. A girl is a daughter all of her life.   —Unknown

I Have a Daughter. What Do I Do with Her?

Dear Sara,

I will never forget the day I was ready to bring Kathleen home from the hospital. The woman in the bed next to me was getting ready to bring her daughter home, and she was so excited as she dressed her daughter in frilly little girl stuff. I loved my daughter, too, but I didn't know what to do with her. I wanted to do the best in the world for her, but I was shut down emotionally and could not even accept myself, much less this child. I remember thinking, "I have one of those (a girl) now. What do I do with her?"

Because I had been an "issue" in my family's life, I never knew the excitement of being a little girl. I never knew acceptance, so I didn't know how to accept my daughter. Kathleen has grown up to be a beautiful, caring, sensitive woman. I wish I could have been more a part of her growing up. Oh, I was there, and I watched from afar, but I didn't feel anything because my feelings had been turned off when I was a baby. I can't go back and redo what I missed, but I can tell her I'm sorry for what we both were robbed of. She is my daughter, and I love her with all my heart. I hope that someday she will be able to forgive me.

God loves you, Sara, and so do I,

Sallie

Only love can be divided endlessly and still not diminish.
—Anne Morrow Lindbergh

Goodbye to My Precious Emily

Dear Sara,

I remember the pain when my granddaughter, Emily, died. It took me a year to let her go. I wrote letters to her telling her how much I loved her. I told her all the things, Sara, that I wanted someone to tell you. I was going to show Emily how special she was and how much she was wanted and loved. Finally, I was going to do it right.

I was going to welcome a little girl into a world filled with love. I was going to let someone into my life for the first time. I was going to feel for the first time. Then my hopes and dreams and my precious Emily were taken home to be with God. I was going to open up, but quickly I shut down again. If I let someone in and they leave or abandon me, the pain is back.

Sara, you know how to heal, and we are healing with God's help. I named Emily; I claimed her, and I healed.

Love,

Sallie

We are only as sick as the secrets we keep. —Unknown

I Uncover That Mental Illness Runs in the Family

Dear Sara,

Many people see little value in sharing family history and medical information with other family members. I see it as an adult responsibility to share such information with future generations because it can help them.

It is with sadness but also with hope that I share this revelation with you. I have uncovered a great deal of information about a form of mental illness that runs in my grandmother's family. I don't see mental illness as anything to be ashamed of. People who are uninformed can say and do things to make people suffering from mental illness feel great shame, but mental illness is a disease or illness like cancer, diabetes, or alcoholism. It just isn't socially acceptable.

I come from a family that kept secrets, secrets that have caused concern and sadness for descendants. I suffer from depression and have been on medication for a few years, and the medication has made a big difference in my life. Through reading and counseling, I have been able to overcome many of my fears. I have a different outlook on life and don't overreact to stressful situations as I once did. But other family members overreacted to situations out of fear and did not pursue proper treatment.

Mental illness may cause you to feel hopeless, have low self-esteem, be fearful and feel that you don't fit in with society. If you have a chemical imbalance in your brain, medication may help you to see more clearly. Sometimes I have felt as though I grew up in a mental institution. The people around me had a strange sense of reality, and many of them did not seek help.

I hope that future generations will seek help early in life so they won't have to live with emotional sadness. But I didn't cause it, and I can't cure it. I can only tell others that it's not a disgrace and that they should never be afraid to seek help. Remember that God has given the gift of knowledge to many in the medical community to help those with mental illness. His Son did not shun or shame people with handicaps. May the wisdom of the Holy Spirit be with everyone so that if they need help, they will search it out and find it. We wish all those who suffer from mental illness God's speed to recovery.

I love you little one,

Sallie

In Step Three, we make an important decision by giving ourselves to God, acknowledging that we need His presence in our lives.

—Ron Ross
Growing Beyond Life's Hurts

Through Al-Anon the Fog Lifts

Dear Sara,

I must study my past to live today and to have hope for tomorrow. This doesn't mean I'm sitting in a "pity party." Study means to learn, gather facts and come to some conclusion. Many people have helped me on my recovery journey.

Through concern for one of my children, I was led to Al-Anon. As I studied and listened in those meetings, the fog I had been living in for forty-eight years started to lift. I was with people who had similar stories to tell, and I could relate to them. I realized that I wasn't crazy. The people at Al-Anon had grown up in non-reality thinking just as I had. Non-reality thinking means trying as hard as you can but not seeing things the way an alcoholic or mentally ill person does. And I had thought that I was the one out of step. I realized there were lots of people who had experienced my reality, and I liked them. I belonged—I had a home—I had a family.

I feel like the people in my family of origin took my brain. They told me what to say, what to do, who I could play with and where I could go. Now I know that's what you call being in a controlled environment. I was like a white lab rat. I was not given choices but rather programmed to react the way they wanted me to.

I remember using my brain for the first time. My grandmother believed that to enter heaven, a person had to be of a certain nationality and religion. A person I admired and who was not of that nationality and religion asked me what I thought about my grandmother's opinion. For the first time I realized that my grandmother's viewpoint was just her opinion, not the gospel truth. And I didn't agree with her opinion. I gave myself permission to have a different opinion. She had controlled everything I did until 1963 when I married Ben. Then I handed the control of my life over to him.

The lights really did not come on until 1990 when someone in Al-Anon told me I was a child of God. God had given me a brain, and He intended me to use it. Wow, what a revelation! The fog lifted. During that first year in Al-Anon I worked on the Third Step of the Twelve-Step Program the most, finding the God of my understanding. I had to leave behind the family of origin who never gave me permission to use my mind. The God of my understanding wears three hats: the Father, the Creator of everything; the Son, the example of how we should lead our lives; and the Holy Spirit, who gives us the gift of wisdom to think. This is when I started to grow up spiritually and emotionally.

God loves you, little girl,

Sallie

Family faces are magic mirrors. Looking at people who belong to us, we see the past, present, and future. We make discoveries about ourselves.
                                                    —Gail Lumet Buckley
                                        The Hornes: An American Family

Retirement from Full-Time Motherhood

Dear Sara,

I was just reading about feelings—those funny things we have, don't know what to do with and don't know what to call. I listened to two friends talking yesterday about leaving their jobs. Both were retiring from full-time careers to be mothers.

I remember when the last one of our kids left home. My husband had adopted a "child" late in life, and that was his business. He said that I could help him run it. So, off I went, with all my mothering skills, into the workplace. Some of my mothering skills came in handy, such as being a good listener to the employees (most of whom I'm old enough to be their mothers), assigning duties and being a hard taskmaster to make people get their work done. Also, I called on such skills as using shame and guilt on people to make them pay their bills and getting sympathy from the people to whom I owed money. You never lose those mothering skills.

Now I'm ready to retire from being a Mom too. I want another life! From all my forty years of mothering experiences, I can take my job training and wisdom and do something with it. What do I want to do is the question. I'm not driven by money. The first forty years didn't pay anything, so why would I want to make money now? You know, Sara, when you retire from being a mom, they don't even give you a gold watch or a party. Maybe we should organize a group and have one big blow-out party. Stop and think about it. We worked 24/7 for all those years with no retirement benefits— no 401K, not even a pat on the back or a congratulations on job well done.

Why did we do it? Some noble people will say we did it because of love. I'm not so sure that's the real answer for me. I did it because it was the thing to do. And I was trying to do it for you, Sara. I wanted subconsciously to do what no one had ever done for me. I raised my children as if I were raising you. I didn't know it at the time, but now I can see that. Everything I did for them was done so they would not feel the pain you experienced growing up. They grew up protected, cared about and watched over. Sara, because I know you and your feelings so well, I think that I was able to be not a perfect mom but a pretty good one. Now that they're gone, I will spend my time caring for you, telling you how special you are and how much I love you. Come on, Sara, let's go out for tea.

Love,

Sallie

Celebrating my fiftieth birthday with Ben and the kids.

You don't get to choose how you're going to die. Or when. You can only decide how you're going to live. Now. —Joan Baez

Goodbye to Sherry

Dear Sara,

My daughter-in-law is gone, but I will always remember her. Thank you, God, for your sweet child, Sherry. She had been on dialysis. We all knew about her illness and the time frame of how long she could be on dialysis, as well as the complications that might take her from us. I know what it's like to have a child die. I've buried one child, and now the life of another has ended.

Life is so precious, and you think it will last forever. People think they will not have to look at saying good-bye. We never know when will be the last time we will hold a loved one, say their name, look into their eyes, or hear their voice. Our life on earth is really a short time, just a journey, a short trip before we join God for the eternal trip. I think about what it says on a Precious Moments figurine, "No more tears beyond this gate."

Earthly tears are tears of the heart as we say good-bye to hopes and dreams. We mortals focus on earthly hopes and dreams, but maybe we should be looking at the dreams of the world we cannot see or dream about. It's a world with no more surgeries, pain, or sadness, a world where loved ones wait for us. Someday we will be together in a world of peace and quiet.

At the heavenly gate stand grandparents, parents, and many small children who have gone on to wait for us to join them. We who are left behind cry because our loved ones are not with us. Maybe we should focus on tears of joy because those who have gone before us are joyfully greeting loved ones they have been waiting for.

On earth we talk to each other on a phone. Sometimes we get a busy signal. But in Heaven we can talk anytime—no waiting, no limited minutes, and no dialing. We can close our eyes and remember the faces of our loved ones, and we can tell them all about our joys and sorrows. If we listen very quietly, we can hear them even now.

Love,

Sallie

No memory is ever alone; it's at the end of a trail of memories, a dozen trails that each have their own associations.

—Louis L'Amour
Ride the River

Time Has Gone By So Fast

Dear Sara,

Today, June 15, 2004, is our forty-first wedding anniversary. Wow! The time has sure gone by fast. The kids are all grown up now and on their own. It seems like a blur going from the apartment on Farragut Road to the house on Illona Drive in Greenhills, Ohio, to St. Cloud, Minnesota. I was always looking for the answer, always searching. I didn't know I was really looking for you, Sara, my inner child, my soul mate, the real me. Everything would have been so different if I'd found you early in my life.

You've taught me compassion as well as shown me the depths of depression and sadness. You've given me hope that things will get better. You've taught me that hope is not a bad word. I used to think that if I hoped and it didn't come true, I would not be able to stand the pain. But you've taught me that God is always with us even when we are not aware that He's there. He will walk with us and give us the courage to get through the toughest of life's journeys. I had to take the journey so that I could look back and say, "See, He will never let me down." God has always been part of my life. If He hadn't been, I would not be here to tell your story, Sara.

I thank God for all of the learning experiences He's given me. Without them, Sara, you would not have a voice. Your voice and your story are so important to tell. There are so many little girls like you in this world, and each is precious in God's sight. For all of them I say, "I will be your voice. All of you are real, and your stories need to be told, too."

I love you, Sara,

Sallie

Chapter Five

The Truth

My Mother's Death and
Moving Beyond the Past

If a family tells a lie long enough, it becomes the truth, and so it was with my family. The only person who did not believe that lie was me. For fifty-six years, I searched for the truth. It came on April 30, 1998. My mother's daughter-in-law, Lisa, called me to come to New Orleans where my mother was dying of cancer. She was being cared for at home by four of her six sons. Lisa said that Margaret was not at peace and that maybe a visit from me might help. I wanted to help her to be at peace with God. When I arrived, she was calling out to special people in her life and wanted to talk to them. For my mother, I played the role of various people who had been part of her life and told her what I was sure she wanted to hear.

Margaret wanted to have a tea party with her daddy, and I could arrange that. She called for her mother, and I took that role as well. In each of the roles, I told her how much each person loved her and was waiting with open arms for her in heaven. I did this so she could be at peace. She also talked about having a baby, a little girl. Since I was her only daughter, I assumed she meant me, but I asked her the baby's name. Then, with an unpleasant face, she said that she must call her Sara. I asked her if she loved the baby. She shook her head, no. I asked if Elizabeth or Dick loved the baby. She again shook her head, no. Then, she said in a very clear voice, "No one likes the baby."

Fifty-five years of hoping to be accepted were ended at that moment. I can honestly say that I had no feelings about the situation. She put into words what I had known all my life but did not want to believe. I lived with a secret and a lie for all those years. I had known the truth but could never prove it. Everyone kept the family secret and the lie going for so long that no one could remember the truth.

* * *

"Mommy Dearest"…

I remember one time after I had my first job, I bought a box of candy for you for Valentine's Day. I put a flower on it and gave it to you. I hoped that you would like it and acknowledge that I had done something nice for you. But you never mentioned my gift.

Later in the week when I went to visit Liz, she told me what a wonderful daughter she had because you had given her a box of candy with a flower on it for Valentine's day.

Liz was angry that I had not gotten her a gift or a card. The gift she got was, of course, the one I had given you. I never said anything, but I never forgot how bad I felt.

* * *

Not all of us live in the beautiful Hallmark world that we see on TV. I wish we did, so people would not need to suffer, be sad or just hang on to survive. I survived physical, sexual, emotional and spiritual abuse as a child, but I'm not the only one who has suffered like this. There are many of us. We have suffered to different degrees and our lives have been significantly affected by our past. But if we can learn from the past and heal, we can have the great life that God intended for us.

It isn't an easy journey, but if we are willing to walk through it, the other side is what heaven is all about. We will have to work very hard to get to the other side. We will need to do the hard work ourselves. No one can do it for us. But, if we are parents, it is the best gift we will ever give our children. It is the best gift we can give ourselves—to be able to trust people, to accept love and to be happy to be alive.

* * *

Why would I make up stories about sexual abuse?

I am asked, "Can you prove it? Are you sure?" Why would I make this up? I don't want this to be my claim to fame. I fear that I will be rejected by the human race and by God. The terrible secret of abuse is still held in my body. I pray no one will be able to see what was done to me. I am still afraid that if people find out, they will ostracize me from society. People don't know what to say. They are so repulsed when they find out what happened to me.

The anger of the act produces an essence that attacks my body and seeps through my skin. I have done nothing wrong, but the essence causes me to think this way. It engulfs my mind with its slime and stench as it tries to suck the life out of my spirit. It goes to my core, my soul, where the real me is.

* * *

Put it behind you. It happened so long ago. Forget about it. Live in the present. That is what people with good intentions tell me—pastors, Christians, people who care about me, people who want my pain to go away, or those who are just too uncomfortable to hear about it. But there has to be a purpose for what I lived through. The purpose, I believe, is to share my story so that others who are walking the same road can have hope and know that God loves them and that He wants them to have a good life.

Today I work with my husband at the business we have owned for over twenty years. I do marketing, bill paying, collections, human resources, praying and whatever else needs to be done for the family business, so I believe that I have made good progress in my recovery.

Adult survivors cope with past abuse in many different ways. I have chosen to speak out publicly about sexual abuse and offer help to other survivors. Ben and I were trained as advocacy workers to offer referral information, assistance, and support to abuse survivors. Also I reactivated Survivors of

Ben and I with Marilyn Van Derbur in 1994.

Incest Anonymous and participated in a group called Survivors Reaching Survivors. I've spoken to various groups, and in 1994 I helped put on a conference on sexual abuse for our community and brought in Marilyn Van Derbur Atler to speak. In 2004, Ben and I established The Sallie Engel Trauma Survivor's Education Fund through the CentraCare Health Foundation to provide ongoing educational programs for doctors and other professionals on how to treat survivors of childhood trauma. These efforts have helped to shift the focus from my traumatic experiences to helping others.

* * *

In the following letters, I reach out to another survivor, express frustration about my own recovery and remind myself that the journey is in God's hands.

I don't think of all the misery but of the beauty that still remains.
—Anne Frank
The Diary of a Young Girl

I Remind Another Survivor of How Special She Is

Dear Sara,

Good morning. Wow, do I have a lot on my mind this morning! You and I both know that we can only do one thing at a time, so let's start out by acknowledging another survivor and her story. You and I both believe some terrible things happened to her when she was little. She does not have to tell us all the details. We can see in her eyes that she is telling the truth. We both know people cannot make up stories about abuse. If it hadn't happened to them, they wouldn't know how to talk about it.

She tried so hard to figure out ways to protect herself. She was always trying to stay covered up so no one could get to her. Now, she is safe, and we believe her. It hurts so much when your own family won't believe you. Mothers and fathers have a hard time choosing between a son who is an abuser and a daughter who is a victim. They don't want to believe it could happen in their family—that their child could hurt another person in such a terrible way, let alone a little sister. People act out in anger. Maybe because he was abused sexually, her brother was trying to prove that he was not gay. He could not take his anger out on another male because that would make him just like his perpetrator.

It doesn't matter why he did what he did. She was hurt, and her self-worth was shattered. Sara, you and I need to remind her how much we love her and how special we think she is. We are so glad God made her. She is caring, smart, beautiful and a wonderful child of God. Maybe if we keep telling her how much we love her, we can help to erase the old tapes that keep playing in her head. We will just keep sending her special thoughts and the Holy Spirit will deliver them.

Love,

Sallie

I have no peace, no quietness; I have no rest, but only turmoil.

—Job 3:26

When Is Someone Going to Help Me?

Dear Sara,

I am so tired of hearing people say I have helped and taught them so much. When is some one going to help me? When am I going to look at someone and say, "Oh, that's the answer I was looking for. Thanks so much. Now I will go on and live a happy life."

I want to get well, and I want to connect to people. I want to look at someone who is further along in recovery and say, "Oh, you have helped me so much." Marilyn Van Derbur Atler was that person for me.

It feels like I am helping others, but I am not getting the help they seem to be getting. They seem happy that they have found the answer. What was the question? Maybe I have the answer, and I just don't know it.

People need to stop telling me I have helped them so much. Don't they see that I'm alone and hurting, and I want to get well too? Yes, God is helping me to get better. I read and study and try to make some sense out of all this stuff, but I just keep working and working, and all I uncover is more work.

I want to be done. I want to say, "I am finished and I am connected to another person. I am well, I am normal and I have a great life." I'm tired of working so hard, and I don't even think I've made a dent in this whole damn mess. I want a life, not just a survival mode.

I know we are not supposed to be greedy, and we are supposed to accept that it will happen in God's time. But maybe it will never happen. Maybe this is as good as it gets. Well, if this is as good as it gets, life is overrated, and I'm sick and tired of the effort.

What the hell is wrong with me? Why can't I connect with anyone? Why can't I trust? What does God want me to see? I don't think I am feeling sorry for myself. I think that I'm just terribly frustrated!

What do you think, Sara?

Love,

Sallie

Just when you think you've graduated from the school of experience,
someone thinks up a new course. —Mary H. Waldrip

It's Not the Destination, It's the Process

Dear Sara,

It's not the destination; it's the process. I need to stop, look around and enjoy what is going on. It's like the little kid in the car who keeps saying, "When do we get there?" I miss the fun of every day because I am not looking around.

I want to be normal, get to the destination. But I am normal because I am right where God wants me to be. I need to enjoy where I am rather than just look where I'm going. The destination is being again in the Father's arms and being at peace.

I will go there soon enough, but He has work for me to do while I'm on earth. I need to be doing the work and enjoying the many blessings He gives me each day.

God's love and peace,

Sallie

Chapter Six

Recovery: God and the Jigsaw Puzzle

Continuing the Spiritual Journey

Recovery is like a jigsaw puzzle for me. I want to be in control and put the outside pieces of the puzzle together first. I want to do it all myself with no help from anyone. I get so locked in on trying to figure out an outside piece, I lose my awareness of what God is trying to tell me. He knows what I need to do. Instead of listening to Him when He gives me a middle piece to the puzzle, I often remain stuck doing things my way and continue to work on an outside piece. This gets me nowhere fast.

God provides a gentle reminder by giving me an inside piece of life's puzzle. I need to pick it up and work on the life experience He hands me. What is that old saying about not seeing the forest for the trees? Life is a process not a destination. Sometimes I can get so into my pre-recovery behavior that I can screw myself right into the ground.

Recently I was struggling with a relationship problem. I was so determined to solve the problem that I was obsessing about it. Someone told me that I was giving this problem too much space in my head. In fact, this problem had the penthouse apartment in my head. I figured out that in this relationship the little kid in me was very much alive. Sara, the little girl, was afraid of this person. I knew in my head that Sallie, the adult, could take him on, and he would not stand a chance. But little Sara, the pre-recovery me, was screaming with fear.

In this situation I was trying to put the outside pieces to life's puzzle together by myself without asking for God's help. God came through as always and gave me a job at work to do that took all of my attention. The job was not something that little Sara could do; it was something that only Sallie, the adult, could do. It took me less then twenty-four hours to take care of this job. Yesterday, when I finished the job, I felt so good about myself. My self-esteem was back up, and I knew I had a brain and that I was a smart person.

I didn't do the job by myself. I asked for help and God provided it. And because I asked for help, even more good came out of it, like "the domino effect." It just kept giving and giving and giving.

I have heard many times in recovery that God will keep blessing you with life experiences until you get the message. Listen to what the life experience is that God wants you to work on, and it will go smoothly. But if you focus on what you think the life experience is, you are in for many problems. God's life experiences build up my self-esteem, mine pull me down. Ask yourself whose life experience you are giving the penthouse in your head—yours or God's.

* * *

These last letters to Sara are a continuation of my spiritual recovery journey and the importance of staying connected to God in this process. My final letter is about what Sara, my inner child, and Sallie, the adult, want others to learn from my experiences and my reflections on life.

[Jesus said], "I have told you these things, so that in me you might have peace. In this world you will have trouble. But take heart! I have overcome the world." —John 16:33

What Would It Be Like to Trust and Relax?

Dear Sara,

What would it feel like to feel connected to someone else? To feel you were part of a family and wanted? To be loved and liked just because you are alive? To not have to do anything special or be anyone special? To not have to work to earn your place in a group or society or prove you are worthy of existence? You would belong because that is how it is. People would not have to give you anything; you would just know you were wanted, and you could feel it. You would never have a thought of not belonging that you would have to keep pushing out of your mind.

That kind of life belongs to *those* people—those who were not abused. For those of us who are survivors, the voices say, "You are not enough; you do not belong, and you are not wanted," and it is stamped with a marker in your brain. You scrub and scrub to erase it, but it still bleeds through and becomes dark and bold and bright.

We survivors must stay strong and connected to God so that the marker in our brain does not take hold. We must keep our strength up, not get sick, not let our guard down or it will attack us—victim, depression, sickness. We can't relax. It is always waiting in the dark, around the corner, ready to attack and pull us down.

"Relax" is a word used in the medical profession quite often. Just relax. How many times have you said it to someone who is upset? Today I went for a relaxing session with my physical therapist. I had been sick for over a week, was very run down and really exhausted. As I crawled up on the table and laid down, I thought that this time I would really relax, as I didn't have the energy to do anything else. I felt myself fall onto the table ready to let all my cares go. His shirt touched my arm, and I reacted the way I always do, with fright. Even when sick, I'm still on guard and always aware of what is happening around me. Relax—that word is not part of my reality. I'm always on guard even with a therapist whom I trust and admire. The trust issue is always in the way. I can't get close to anyone or trust anyone because the fear of being hurt is so strong. I never feel safe.

Sara, I think that *those* people must be able to relax, and it must be so enjoyable. Sleeping pills let me sleep, but no pill can let me relax. To relax I must be able to trust that the darkness won't get me and that I can be at peace. Someday, I will know that joy of not having to be on guard. That is what my heaven is going to be like.

Love,

Sallie

Many are the plans in a man's heart, but it is the Lord's purpose that prevails. —Proverbs 19:21

Let Go of Being So Responsible

Dear Sara,

I have chest pains. What's going on? Being responsible, trying to keep peace and figuring out how to manage everything is overwhelming. In fact, being responsible is a real pain in the backside.

When you were growing up, Sara, living in the confusion of non-responsible adults was a really scary situation. You could never relax. You always had to be alert and on guard. You couldn't count on anyone to help you out, answer your questions, or take care of you. You were alone in a great big, confusing, out-of-control mess. Somehow you took on the job of trying to hold everything together. You really couldn't do it, and so you felt bad. You felt that if you had just tried harder or been smarter, you could have held things together, and life would have been good.

You became a leader by default because a bunch of adults didn't want to grow up and take responsibility for the mess they had created. Being thrown into a motherhood role when you were just a kid yourself was scary. No one died under your care, so that is something to your credit. But you felt very guilty and thought that if you had just paid better attention and worked harder, you could have turned everything around.

Sara, I know you tried to keep the family together, and I give you credit for being a hard worker. You did the best you could with the tools you had at the time. How the adults in your life acted and what they did was about them and not about you.

We all need to remember that God is in charge, and He expects us to try to do our part, but He does not expect us to do His job. We need to look at what is God's job, and what is our responsibility. Maybe, we need to let go of being so responsible. We can do what we can and then walk away. We can see how God wants it to turn out because we know He has the best plan.

Love,

Sallie

Your kingdom come, your will be done on earth as in heaven.
—Matthew 6:10

God's Will Be Done

Dear Sara,

I am aware of a wall around me and how I don't want to feel pain. If I have hope, then I set myself up for pain. If I pray, I pray for God's will to be done. If I ask for something from God, and it's not His will, I might be disappointed. If I pray for God to watch over someone, I don't ask Him to do something. I thank God for His many blessings, but I don't ask God for something I want. It's better to ask for the strength to see His will be done.

If I get my hopes up or get excited, I'll cry if I'm disappointed. Be realistic, I tell myself. I will receive what God wants me to have when He wants me to have it. I should be satisfied with what He gives me and what I learn from the experiences He blesses me with. Once I accept that I am here on earth to learn to appreciate and know God, then I can have peace and calm.

Heaven is where pain and suffering no longer roam. Life on earth has a beginning and an end. People and situations will not last forever, so I should not get too attached or excited. I should go with the change, the learning experiences, and the fact that I am growing and beginning to understand God's plan. If I free anger and stress from my body and be childlike in my thinking, I'll be at peace. Have I figured life out, or do I just not want to feel? Maybe, I just don't know how to feel anymore?

Ben and I have a big job we've been working on for over a year at the office. I am not stressed because I know a new learning experience is just around the corner. Life is a series of learning experiences. This one job is not going to be an answer to the problems of the business. It's not a solution; it's just a temporary fix. Life is a lot of work, so I'll just put one foot in front of the other and keep on moving.

I wonder if I need my meds changed?

Love,

Sallie

A man's heart plans his way, But the Lord directs his steps.
—Proverbs 16:9

All Experiences Have a Message

Dear Sara,

How are you today? You seem to be sitting very quietly. You don't seem happy or sad, just very quiet. Maybe it's like waiting for the next life experience to come along or as some say, waiting for the other shoe to drop. I guess my prayer today would be: "Dear God, please give me the strength to get through whatever you have planned. So many of your plans take a lot of work and energy."

Today I can do a little cleaning and tidy up the messes that have been lying around for some time. It can be a "clean my room day." But maybe I should save my energy for my next assignment. I'll bet God has a learning experience in store for me. Each experience has a message, and God's message is always so interesting.

I can walk a journey, and when I come out on the other side, I see what God wants me to see. I can't see the message until I walk the journey. Life is not like a crystal ball because I can't see the future. I can't plan for the future. It's a daily walk—a spiritual journey filled with joy and sorrow. I take it each day as it comes. I really can't plan for it because I don't have a clue what is going to come my way. I live life moment by moment, and then I look back and say, "Oh, now I see what the plan was."

Sara, when will I ever learn to keep my mouth shut and not be so judgmental? Sometimes, a picture is not what it seems to be, and people are not who we think they are. It is wise to be cautious. We don't know someone else's journey. We need to find out what that person's journey is, and then we can figure out what we need to do.

Love,

Sallie

Let everything that has breath praise the Lord . . .

—Psalm 149:7

God Supplies Me with All My Needs

Dear Sara,

I thank God for the many blessings He has given me —for my husband who has stood by me on my journey and recovery—for my children and grandchildren and the other people who have been such an important part of my life.

I thank God for my health, my home, the beautiful day, flowers, birds, Toby (my dog), my sight, and so much more. God is so good. He supplies me with everything I need each day. I want to show my appreciation for His love by encouraging people on their journey to recovery. I ask God to please enlighten me as to what He wants me to do.

Love,

Sallie

Look not mournfully into the past. It comes not back again. Wisely improve the present. It is thine. Go forth to meet the shadowy future, without fear. —Henry Wadsworth Longfellow

Accept God's Journey for You and You Will Find Peace

Dear Sara,

I have come a long way with God's help. I am on the right track now. I am working and accepting what God has planned for me. It's not a destination; it's a journey. And the journey is not without pain and fear. But if I remember that God has not let me down so far, life is easier. He will not let me remember anything we can't handle together. Life is just one experience after another. If I stay in the experience, I learn about me. In learning about myself, I'm able to help others to see God. That is what the journey is all about. If I accept the journey, I will be at peace. If I fight the journey, I will have no peace, and the pain will last longer and longer.

My past haunts me, but if I am willing to uncover it, I can live today and have hope for tomorrow. When I focus on the destination, I become frustrated. I've mistakenly thought that if I am a good person and if I try not to hurt anyone or anything, I will be rewarded. I'm being rewarded but not with the rewards I thought I would get. God expects us to be on earth to help and support our fellow man. When people thank me for helping them, that is a reward from God. He is showing me that I'm doing the right thing. God is the teacher; I'm the student. And if I tutor others in God's goodness, I'm being a good student.

Moses wandered forty years in the desert looking for the Promised Land. I have wandered sixty-one years on this earth looking for joy, peace and happiness. When I accept God's will, I have those things if I reach out for them and let them into my soul. Trusting people is very difficult for me because of being hurt. Sharing my story and listening to others are ways of letting people in.

Will I ever get over the loneliness and feeling of not being connected to anyone or anything? My guard is always up even with people I know, admire and love. I want to trust, but, as hard as I try, it doesn't happen. My faith in God is strong. I believe that He is my friend—someone who is always part of my life and is always available. God is forever. Human beings change their minds, leave and die.

Sometimes I wonder if it's a boundary or a wall that I feel between others and myself. What is the feeling I am looking for? Is it being connected? What does that feel like? What is a healthy way of being connected? I think it's knowing that I will not hurt you and you will not hurt me. Being connected is reaching out—letting others share their pain and joy and accepting them right where they are. There is a joy when you can be open and honest with others. Being open and honest can bring peace, joy, love and serenity.

God's peace to you,

Sallie

Life's unfairness is not irrevocable; we can help balance the scales for others, if not always for ourselves. —Hubert H. Humphrey

My Experiences Are Not Unique

Dear Sara,

What do I want to tell people? I want to tell them that the pain and crazy feelings they have can subside and even go away. They can have peace, if they are willing to do their work. It's not easy, but it's well worth it. There are people who will support you in your community. You can have a better life if you nurture the small child inside that needs to be heard.

Many people will never understand the demons that have plagued me over the years. I have been greatly affected by my childhood experiences. I realize these experiences, though neither unique nor pleasant, have taught me a great deal. I have met many other women and men who have had similar experiences. My hope is to encourage them and let them know that life can be better if they are willing to study their past so they can live today and have hope for tomorrow. Because God let me suppress so much of my past, all of my energy went into keeping it hidden away. I didn't intentionally do this. It was my survival technique. As I found myself in a safe place with a caring supportive husband and good medical people, I was able to let the past come out. I call it "getting my brain back."

The neglect and abuse of my childhood took my brain. It caused a cloud of depression to cover my life. Having it lifted is like seeing daylight for the first time. I'm seeing the world in an entirely different way. As I understand why I saw the world in a haze, the fog clears, and I join the human race. When I see other wounded people who are still in the fog, I know that they will take this spiritual journey in their own time and in their own way. I hope that in some way I can encourage them to believe that God wants us to have all the gifts of the Holy Spirit.

I hope that our message will help others, Sara. If it does, our journey will have been worth the pain.

Love,

Sallie

Chapter Seven

A Home at Last

Sara Finds Peace

During the many years of my recovery journey, I have nurtured Sara, my wounded inner child, and offered her a safe haven. Now she has split off and found a home. She is the little girl whose photograph once hung in her grandparents' home, then her mother's home, and now hangs above the fireplace mantle in my home. At last Sara has a home where she is loved, accepted and wanted. Sara is no longer a lost and wandering soul. She is at peace and a strong and beautiful child of God.

Sara needed to be heard, and she has taught me so much. She had many stories to tell me, stories that only she knew. There are many children like Sara—lost souls who are crying out and wandering this earth looking for a home. I have listened to Sara, grown to love her, to care about her and to respect her. I would not be the woman I am today if it had not been for her strength. I hope that you have appreciated getting to know her. Maybe you, too, will find the lost child in you. God's love and peace to each of you,

Sallie Engel

Sallie C. Engel
July 2004

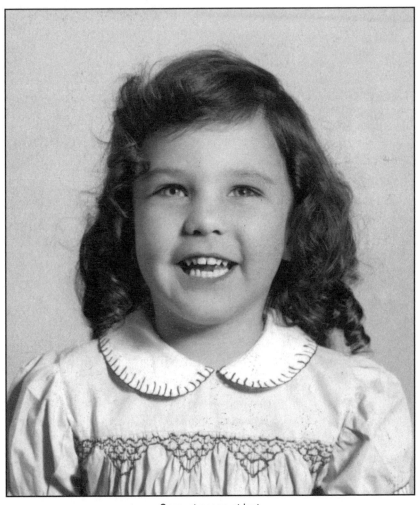
Sara, at peace at last.

Our prayers are answered not when we are given what we ask but when we are challenged to be what we can be.

—Morris Adler

Epilogue to My Readers

August 2004

Now I'm on another journey. In November 2003 I didn't feel well, was becoming very jaundiced and was in terrible pain. I sought medical care and even made a couple of trips to the emergency room. I went to the University of Minnesota Hospital, Hennepin County Medical Center and then spent three days at the Mayo Clinic just before Christmas. By Christmas we had the word—CANCER—pancreatic cancer. We were told that it was not curable. Chemotherapy and radiation were started, and I was given pain medication.

One doctor said I had a year and a half to live, another said a year and finally the last one said six months. But I have a lot of people praying for me, and I think that God may have something else in mind. So, until God calls me home, I've been doing what I like to do—like having coffee with friends and meeting Ben for lunch. If I die in a day or in five thousand days, I need to focus and make the best of each day.

Many people whose lives have touched mine have e-mailed me, sent a card, cooked a meal, driven me to a doctor's appointment, prayed with me or just held my hand and said they care. I know I'm loved by God and by my earthly community. God's plan may be painful, but the many things learned from His lessons are worth the price and effort.

God's love and peace to each of you,

Ben and I, August 2004.

September 2004

Dear Reader,

 After a valiant fight, Sallie died on Saturday, September 18, 2004, at about 5:25 p.m. She was very active until July 15, 2004. At that time she became unable to leave home and began receiving hospice services. She continued to be active at home until Wednesday, September 15. Her last days were very peaceful with very little pain. She died at home with all of her family with her.

God's Peace,

Les (Ben) Engel

Part Two

Resources to Help in
Working with Survivors

Relationships help us define who we are
and what we can become.
Most of us can trace our successes
to pivotal relationships.

—Donald O. Clifton and Paula Nelson
Soar with Your Strengths

Chapter Eight

From the Health Care Professionals' Perspective

I began working on the traumas of my childhood in 1991 and found some excellent health care professionals who helped me immensely. But I had to search them out, and with God's help was fortunate in finding them. A person can't just look in the phone book under "my-life-is-a-mess specialist" and find a complete listing.

First I had to recognize that emotional, spiritual, physical and sexual abuse had affected me. Then I had to identify how I had been affected. Some health care professionals were willing to learn about the effects of childhood trauma while others were not. It takes a special type of health care professional to understand that different physical systems can be affected by traumas from the past. I don't think that they are given adequate training in how past traumas can affect people in the present.

Those who work in the healing professions have said that they've learned a lot about helping other survivors of trauma as they've worked with me. The contributions in this chapter are from some of these very special health care professionals. The final contribution is a letter from my pastor who provided the spiritual support in my healing journey.

A Psychologist's Perspective

Heroic Healing

I met Sallie on January 17, 1991. She wrote on the intake form: "I want to remember what happened so I can better understand why I have as much fear as I do."

I remember saying to her that we should be able to take care of that in about six months. Over the years, we've joked about that overly optimistic prediction.

I have met a lot of heroes in my office. Sallie is at the top of my list. Her fierce determination to heal, to face what needed to be faced and learn what needed to be learned always inspired me. I don't know if I've ever seen anyone work so hard in therapy, and with such tenacity. She continues to inspire as I see her gracefulness in surrendering to God's will.

Much of the first few years of our work together focused on unraveling the story of her sexual, physical and emotional abuse. Since much of the abuse occurred before Sallie had words, experiences were stored and expressed in the body. Intense headaches and pain in her face, arm, shoulder, chest, and legs shouted the tale of abuse. Visual memories of assaults in her crib flashed before her. It takes extraordinary courage to retrieve such horrific memories. And that's just what she did.

As her story emerged, it became clear that she was a rejected and resented child—a target for the hostility of those around her, an object, an "it." In family-systems theory, she was the classic scapegoat.

There is no way for an abused and depersonalized child to avoid internalizing this attitude. So often, in the early years of our work, Sallie would approach herself as a project, a broken object that needed fixing. As an "it," she had no right to feel and very little sense of her own subjectivity as a unique person. She was either useful or useless. And, if useless, she expected to be discarded.

In the world of her younger days, if she claimed personhood, the basic right to have feelings (like anger, for example), she felt sure to be banished. She grew so accomplished at disconnecting and splitting off from her feeling self that it took years of work for her to learn to identify, accept and express feelings. At first, the only way to know she was angry was to notice her head and shoulder pain, which often signaled anger.

The journey from "it" to unique personhood and beloved child of God was long and arduous. The intense shame of an abused child, that powerful sense of being somehow defective, is a huge obstacle. Sallie researched and read and studied. Marilyn VanDerbur Atler taught her that secrecy feeds the shame. So, Sallie spoke out, went public, self-disclosed, and extended herself to other survivors. Her groups and her advocacy have helped hundreds in their healing. Her nurturing of others has helped her heal, as well.

For years, we worked with the wounded, inner child —inviting this young part to come forth, inviting her to be seen and heard in a holding environment of unconditional acceptance. Sallie found a Raggedy Ann to carry with her for a while, as a way to make concrete the self-nurturing she was learning. On behalf of her younger self, and at times from the perspective of her younger self, she wrote her abusers, letting her feelings flow. She became the mom for herself that she never had. The grown-up Sallie, highly competent and quite intelligent, offered the wounded girl the warm welcome and safe haven she deserved. Eventually, that wounded part—so split off—found her home.

Throughout this entire, arduous journey toward healing and wholeness, Sallie enjoyed (and sometimes didn't enjoy, but at least experienced) the steady and sturdy companionship of her husband, Les, the other hero of this story. He came to most of her sessions, witnessed countless flashbacks and dissociative episodes where the wounded child came forth in all her panic and pain, her anger and anguish. He remained steadfast through it all, a true partner in healing. As part of her heroic effort, Sallie reached out to other healers—physicians, physical therapists, massage therapists, chiropractors—wonderful healers, who helped tremendously. She reached out to friends and other survivors. And she reached out to God and church, and a special pastor.

The human connection really helped. In describing her human helpers, Sallie sometimes used the expression "God with skin on." I believe she understood that the miracle of her healing was divine in origin.

Sallie opened herself to God's love, the ultimate antidote to shame. In that Presence, there is nothing that can't be healed. Sallie knows this. She has experienced it and has taught me about it—because sometimes I forget.

It's now mid-July 2004. Last week, I sat with Sallie on three different evenings. We talked some, but mostly I just held her hand. I'm so touched by her, by her faith, and by her peaceful surrender. She is at peace. It flows through her face and through her eyes and through the hand I'm holding. I don't know how much longer her journey will last. I do know that I am in the presence of a heroic, healed being.

And her healing heals us.

James Bryer, Ph.D.

A Physical Therapist's Perspective

I first met Sallie Engel about 1990 in my work as a physical therapist. She was referred by one of the local physicians for treatment of severe shoulder pain. He wanted her seen that day because he didn't have any good ideas on how to treat her. As a physical therapist, my normal regimen with new patients was to go over their medical history, review the doctor's findings and then discuss the patient's symptoms—when the problem started, where the pain was, what made it better or worse. I would proceed with a physical examination to check range of motion of involved joints, strength of muscles, and tenderness to touch, among other things. Then I would proceed to a treatment program, which might consist of using modalities such as ultrasound, electric stimulation or massage. I would then place the patient on some type of home exercises and talk about what he or she should or should not be doing at home.

When Sallie came in, I looked over her chart, went through the doctor's report, introduced myself and started to take her history. And that's when my life changed. The ten minutes I had planned to spend on her history turned into forty-five minutes as I sat back and listened in amazement to some of the experiences she had been through. By the time my next patient arrived, I hadn't even started Sallie's physical exam, let alone recommended a treatment. I gave her a few suggestions on what to try, and then scheduled her for a more complete evaluation on the following day. To my amazement, she came back the next day feeling much better, and somehow she was putting me up on a pedestal, suggesting that I was some great therapist while I had been thinking just the opposite.

Since then I have seen Sallie for many different conditions, and I have found that simply listening has been one effective way of treating her as a survivor of childhood sexual abuse. Sallie and I have developed a relationship of trust, in which I can treat her for a variety of conditions, some physical problems and some forms of body memory trauma relating back to her childhood sexual abuse. Together we have found a treatment plan that works for her.

Sallie has educated me on many aspects of sexual abuse and how common it is. She has helped me to become a better physical therapist, especially with patients who are survivors of childhood sexual abuse. I now know how important it is to take the time to listen and really communicate with the survivor, to work together to devise a treatment plan, and to schedule appointments at lunchtime or at the end of the day so the patient doesn't feel rushed. Also, I try to explain the techniques physical therapists use, especially if it is necessary to touch the patient in sensitive areas. And last but certainly not least, I try to help if a patient is having a flashback. I let her/him know that this is a safe place.

If you have never had the opportunity to meet and talk with Sallie, you're a missing a lot. She has a unique and interesting way of making you a better person. Besides making me a better physical therapist, she has made me a better husband and family man and has strengthened my faith in God. I will be dedicating part of my life now to helping other health care professionals develop a better understanding of survivors of sexual abuse.

Steve Carr

A Chiropractor's Perspective

I first met Sallie in the fall of 2002. She was referred to me by another health care provider for acupuncture for pain control. I felt like God had placed her in my office for multiple reasons.

From the first meeting, I knew that this experience was going to be something different because of her openness in discussing her abuse, her candid approach as to how I could help her, and her ability to teach me how I could best help other survivors. I am honored to be one of the doctors in her life.

The other very significant aspect of our visits was that she was always concerned about how I was doing. She would often say, "Well, how are you today?" Sallie was very instrumental in my growth as a person. She has this incredible way of reaching out to you and getting to the point without offending you.

Knowing Sallie has changed the way I deal with survivors because I am aware that they are out there and that very often I need to, very gently, open the door to options for the survivor. Sallie has also made me aware of resources for the abuse survivor and how to be a safe source for this discussion.

One of my favorite "Sallieisms" is, "When the student is ready the teacher will come." This statement has changed the way I parent, my relationship with patients, staff, and friends. I have learned to be patient with the process and to allow people to learn when they are ready, but I believe that God has placed me in their pathway for a reason. I am part of the pathway; I pray and then let God direct the rest of the journey.

Sallie is one of those "once in a life time people." She has been blessed, through her pain, to touch and affect each one of us in a special way. She has been a powerful influence in my life, and I pray I can carry her message to all the people I come in contact with.

Jeff Varner

A Pastor's Perspective

Dear Sallie,

    I am excited about your book and your plan to make this book not only a historical account of your life as a survivor of sexual abuse, but also a resource to help health care professionals in working with sexual abuse survivors. Since materials and research on this topic are limited, because sexual abuse has been hidden in our culture, your forthrightness in telling your story is significant, and to pass this story on to others is commendable.

    To the best of my recollection, you and Les became members of Atonement Lutheran Church in 1990. Because you were uncertain of your baptism, you were baptized in 1992, at which time you affirmed your faith in Christ as Lord and Savior. As a child of God you accepted God's unconditional love for you, God's forgiveness and God's grace to support your life journey.

    As our pastor/parishioner relationship grew, I began to realize the significant burden you were carrying and how devastating sexual abuse is to the lives of those whose innocence and trust is violated by an abuser. As you opened your life to me and I began to see your daily struggle at survival, my understanding and compassion grew not only for you, but for all survivors of sexual abuse.

    The Holy Spirit of God was working in your life through your daily struggle, and it took focus in your passion to reach out and help other survivors. I vividly remember the day you sat in my office and told me you wanted to begin helping survivors through developing and leading support groups. In the early days, those groups took form around Vern Bittner's book, *You Can Help with Your Healing*. Later it took expression in Twelve Step groups and numerous other groups.

When we began the Befriender Program at Atonement, I asked you to take the training, and you obliged. Being exposed to the listening ministry approach opened the next door of your journey to help others. Your new ministry was not only to create a safe culture for survivors in a small group, but to compassionately coach them along their journey to recovery. These one-on-one relationships began to develop throughout the community, and I remember the day you brought in your business cards and told me your office was at Starbuck's at Barnes and Noble Booksellers.

When I think of all the parishioners I have served in my many years of ministry, no one has given me more books to read than Sallie Engel. From Twelve Step books to personal testimonies on sexual abuse and survival to daily devotional materials for survivors, I have read them. And I can honestly say that my reading and my personal interaction with you, Sallie, have enriched my ministry beyond measure.

Sallie, once again God is leading you in another direction as you battle with cancer. If I had my say in all of this, it would be that you live to be a cancer survivor. But I know that your future is not mine to call. But I do know that God has a purpose in all that happens, and we are baptized and called to live and die in that trust relationship, knowing that in all things God works for the good of those who love Him.

In the end, we have the promise from God that we will become a new creation. In the Kingdom of God "the lamb at the center of the throne will be our shepherd, and God will guide us to the springs of the water of life, and God will wipe away every tear from our eyes" (Revelation 7:17).

And, Sallie, your survival days will be over once and for all!
God will give you and all believers in Christ eternal peace.

Thank you, Sallie, for allowing me to minister to you
during your life journey, and thank you for all you have done
to point the way for others. Remember, God does not judge,
God loves you!

Sincerely in Christ,

Gerald M. Staehling
Pastor

Letters to Sara

Chapter Nine

Survivors Speak Out

I have spoken to many survivors over the years. Those of us who are survivors of childhood sexual abuse often have a variety of health problems and receive care from many health care professionals. Some of the long-term effects we may be struggling with are posttraumatic stress disorder, multiple personalities or addictions to food. As noted in a Survivors of Incest Anonymous, Inc. (SIA) brochure called *To: The Health Care Professional, From: Your Patient, The Survivor of Sexual Child Abuse*, many of us have neglected our own health care because we fear authority figures and feel vulnerable and anxious during appointments. In addition, if an examination triggers memories or flashbacks of the abuse, we worry about not being in control. The manner in which we are treated can greatly affect our recovery. Here are some suggestions for health care professionals from the SIA brochure.

1. Don't be afraid to ask questions. There is no right way to facilitate disclosure of childhood sexual abuse, so ask an open-ended question such as, "Is there anything else you feel I should know before we begin?" Trust is a central issue for us, as we want to be believed and not judged. If the question prompts disclosure of past abuse, an appropriate response is: "I'm sorry that happened to you. It wasn't your fault."

2. Ask if help has been received to work through issues surrounding the abuse. If not, be prepared to provide a list of mental health professionals experienced in the treatment of sexual abuse. Ask what you can do to make our appointments easier and less frightening. Explain what to expect during each step of the procedure or examination.

3. In the initial visit discuss what you can do to help if a flashback occurs. Touching us may make matters worse. Some of us find that deep breathing exercises help us return to the present. Others need to be held and comforted as one would a terrified child. Some of us need only to be told we are safe in your office and what we are experiencing is not happening now.

4. Let us set the pace of the examination. Encourage us to talk about our fears. Treat us with sensitivity while being attentive to boundaries and the effects of traumatic experiences on the body. If we need it and it's possible, take a break during an exam or procedure. If necessary, reschedule another appointment to complete the examination. Consider scheduling us at the end of the day to allow extra time.

5. Provide a safe and comfortable environment for survivors. According to researchers Schachter, Rodamsky, Stalker and Teram in "How can health professionals promote healing?" on the Canadian Family Physician website (www.cfpc.ca), women survivors said that, first and foremost, they need to feel safe when interacting with health care professionals. They encouraged physicians to consider factors which affect the sense of safety in their office environment, such as:

> Are your exam rooms soundproof?
> Do you provide a third person to be present during exams?
> Do you ask the survivor to remove her clothing before you talk to her?
> Do you ask permission to examine each time?
> Do you allow plenty of time for listening?
> Do you involve the survivor in the decision making process?

6. Become informed about abuse as a health issue. It can affect many systems of the body. Be knowledgeable about coordinating care so you can refer a survivor with chronic pain to other sensitive health care professionals.

As survivors, we are at risk for chronic pain and long-term medical problems. We agree with the Canadian study survivors who said they "want safe, accepting environments and sensitive, informed health professionals with whom to work in partnership on all their health concerns."

God's peace to you,

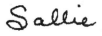

Additional Resourses

Allender, Dr. Dan B., *The Wounded Heart*, Colorado: Navpress, 1995.

Aninscough, Carolyn and Kay Toon, *Surviving Childhood Sexual Abuse, Practical Self-Help for Adults who were Sexually Abused as Children*, Cambridge, MA: Fisher Books, 2000.

Bass, Thornton, *I Never Told Anyone: Writings by Women Survivors of Child Sexual Abuse*, New York: Harper and Row Publishers, 1983.

Beattie, Melody, *Beyond Codependency*, New York: Harper and Row Publishers, 1989.

Beattie, *Melody, Choices*, New York: Harper and Row Publishers, 2002.

Beattie, Melody, *Codependent No More*, New York: Harper and Row Publishers, 1987.

Beattie, Melody, *More Language of Letting Go*, Minneapolis: Hazelden, 2000.

Beattie, Melody, *Playing It by Heart*, Minneapolis: Hazelden, 1999.

Beattie, Melody, *Talk, Trust, and Feel*, New York: Ballantine Books, 1991.

Beattie, Melody, *The Language of Letting Go*, New York: MJF Books, 1990.

Beattie, Melody, *The Lessons of Love*, New York: Harper and Row Publishers, 1961.

Berne, Katrina H., *Running on Empty*, Alameda, CA: Hunter House, 1992.

Black, Claudia, *It Will Never Happen to Me! Children of Alcoholics,* Denver: MAC Publishing, 1981.

Brown, Abigail, *And Don't Tell Anyone, Healing from Incest Through Poetry and Art*, St. Cloud: North Star Press of St. Cloud, Inc., 1997.

Carder, Dave, *Secrets of Your Family Tree*, Chicago: Moody Bible Institute, 1991.

Carnes, Patrick, *Out of the Shadows*, Minneapolis: Hazelden, 1992.

Chopra, Deepak, *Journey into Healing*, New York: Hannony Books, 1994.

Clarke, Jean Illsley, *Self-Esteem: A Family Affair,* Minneapolis: Winston Press, 1978.

Cloud, Dr. Henry and Dr. John Townsend, *Safe People*, Grand Rapids, MI: Zondervan Publishing House, 1995.

Cocola, Nancy Wasserman, *Six in the Bed*, New York: Perigee Books, 1997.

Donoghue, Paul J. and Mary E. Siegel, *Sick and Tired of Feeling Sick and Tired*, New York: WW. Norton and Company, 1992.

Engel, Beverly, *Raising Your Sexual Self-Esteem*, New York: Ballantine Books, 1995.

Engel, Beverly, *The Right to Innocence*, New York: Ivy Books, 1989.

Flaherty, Sandra, *Woman Why Do You Weep*, Spirituality for Survivors of Childhood Sexual Abuse, Mahwah, NJ: Paulist Press, 1992.

Gil, Iliana, *Outgrowing the Pain*, New York: Dell Publishing, 1983.

Hallowell, Edward M. and John Ratey, *Driven to Distraction*, New York: Touch Stone, 1994.

Hart, Dr. Archibald D., *Dark Clouds Silver Linings*, Colorado: Focus on the Family Publishers, 1993.

Heitritter, Lynn and Jeanette Vought, *Helping Victims of Sexual Abuse, A Sensitive, Biblical Guide for Counselors*, Victims and Families. Minneapolis: Bethany House Publishers, 1989.

Hicks, Robert, *Failure to Scream*, Nashville: Thomas Nelson Publishers, 1993.

Jampolsky, Gerald, *Goodbye to Guilt, Releasing Fear through Forgiveness*, New York: Bantam Books, 1985.

Kushner, Harold S., *When Bad Things Happen to Good People*, New York: Avon Books, 1973.

Kushner, Harold S., *Who Needs God*, New York: Pocket Books, 1989.

Leman, Dr. Kevin and Randy Carlson, *Unlocking the Secrets of Your Childhood Memories,* Nashville: Thomas Nelson Publishers, 1989.

Lewis, C.S.,*A Grief Observed*, New York: Harper and Row Publishers, 1961.

Lowen, Alexander, *The Betrayal of the Body*, New York: MacMillian, 1967.

Maltz, Wendy, *The Sexual Healing Journey*, New York: Harper and Row Publishers, 1992.

Meier, MD, Paul and Robert Wise, Ph.D., *Windows of the Soul*, Nashville: Thomas Nelson Publishers, 1995.

Mellody, Pia, *Facing Codependence*, New York: Harper and Row Publishers, 1989.

Minirth, Frank, *Miracle Drugs*, Nashville: Thomas Nelson Publishers, 1995.

Minirth, Frank, *The Power of Memories*, Nashville: Thomas Nelson Publishers, 1995.

Minirth, Dr. Frank and Dr. Paul Meier, *Love Hunger*, Nashville: Thomas Nelson Publishers, 1990.

Nakken, Craig, *The Addictive Personality*, Minneapolis: Hazelden, 1988. Ogilvie, Lloyd J., Climbing the Rainbow, Dallas: Word Publishing, 1993.

Parkinson, Frank, *Post-Trauma Stress*, Tucson: Fisher Books, 1993.

Ross, Ron, *Growing Beyond Life's Hurts, A Christ-centered Recovery Handbook*. Stony Point, NC: Stony Point Christian Publications, 1990.

Rubin, Theodore Isaac, *The Angry Book*, New York: MacMillian, 1969.

Seamands, David A., *Putting Away Childish Things*, Wheaton, IL: Victor Books, 1984.

Slaikeu, Dr. Karl A. and Steve Lawhead, *Up from the Ashes*, Grand Rapids, MI: Zondervan Publishing House, 1990.

Stanley, Charles, *Becoming Emotionally Whole*, Nashville: Thomas Nelson Publishers, 1996.

Vannoy, Steven W., *The Ten Greatest Gifts I Give My Children*, New York: Fireside, 1994.

Van Derbur, Marilyn, *A Story of Hope*, VHS. Denver

VanDerbur, Marilyn, *Miss America By Day, Lesson Learned from Ultimate Betrayals And Unconditional Love*, Denver: Oak Hill Ridge Press, 2003.

Van Derbur, Marilyn, *Once Can Hurt a Lifetime*, VHS. Washington, DC: One Voice, 1994.

Wegscheider, Don, *If Only My Family Understood Me*, Minneapolis: CompCare Publishers, 1979.

Wilson, Sandra D., *Hurt People Hurt People*, Nashville: Thomas Nelson Publishers, 1993.

Wilson, Sandra D., *Released from Shame*, Downers Grove, IL: InterVarsity Press, 1990.

Woititz, Janet G., *Healing Your Sexual Self,* Deerfield, FL: Health Communications, 1989.

Sallie's Legacy

I had the pleasure of meeting Sallie when she was working with the CentraCare Health Foundation to establish the Sallie Engel Trauma Survivor's Education fund.

Her struggle to overcome the trauma of her childhood and her courageous battle with cancer is an inspiration to us all. Her spirit of giving will continue through her fund to provide programs, training, and education for medical professionals and caregivers who work with survivors of trauma.

As Pearl S. Buck said, "We learn as much from sorrow as from joy, as much from illness as from health, from handicap as from advantage—and indeed perhaps more."

Sallie's legacy will be teaching people how to help trauma survivors and teaching trauma survivors how to begin the healing process.

Thank you, Sallie, for this generous gift and for sharing of yourself."

—Terry Pladson, M.D.
CentraCare Health System President

A Final Tribute from Family and Friends . . .

Sallie believed in going out and serving many people in her community. Here she is in March 1989 dressed in her daffodil costume ready to sell daffodils for the American Cancer Society. She worked on this annual sale for fourteen years.

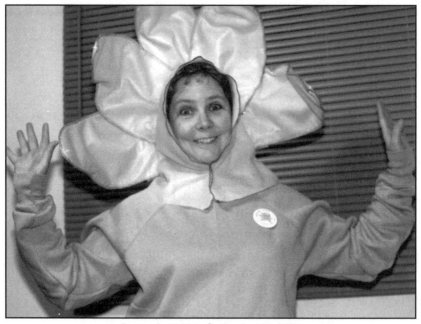

August 6, 1942 to September 18, 2004

Well done, good and faithful servant . . .
enter into the joy of your master.
—Matthew 25:23